Morning Glories
and
Moonflowers

A GUIDE TO CLIMBING, TRAILING, AND
CASCADING PLANTS

by Anne Halpin

Simon & Schuster

NEW YORK LONDON TORONTO SYDNEY TOKYO SINGAPORE

SIMON & SCHUSTER
Rockefeller Center
1230 Avenue of the Americas
New York, NY 10020

Design by Sisco & Evans, Ltd.

Photography credits:
Elvin McDonald: pages 11, 15, 24, 31, 34, 36, 38, 40, 48, 55, 64, 66, 68, 69, 72, 73, 78, 79, 80, 85, 87, 88, 89, 93
Tom Moyer: pages 10, 14, 17, 18 (left), 23, 28, 29, 30, 35, 44, 45, 46, 47, 51, 52, 54, 57, 60, 71, 76, 81, 90, 91
Dency Kane: pages 8, 12, 18 (top), 21, 26, 27, 56, 75
Anne Halpin: pages 16, 20, 25, 33, 37, 43, 59, 61, 63, 82, 83, 92

10 9 8 7 6 5 4 3 2 1

Library of Congress Cataloging-in-Publication Data
Halpin, Anne Moyer.
    Morning glories and moonflowers : a guide to climbing, trailing, and cascading plants / Anne Halpin.
        p. cm.
    Includes index.
        1. Ornamental climbing plants. I. Title
SB427.H35 1996   95-12072
635.9'74—dc20   CIP

ISBN 0-684-81169-3

Contents

Introduction

When I first moved to the Hamptons, my husband-to-be and I rented a tiny cottage overlooking a canal.
There wasn't much space for a garden, but of course I started one, and by summer the front of the cottage was lush
with flowers, vegetables, and herbs.

The most rewarding plants in that small garden were the Morning glories and moonflowers
that I trained on vertical strings along the front and sides of the tiny porch.

The vines, with their heart-shaped green leaves, created some shade and privacy on the porch.
And the flowers were magical.

Big blue morning glories the color of the summer sky opened at dawn.
Although each blossom lasted for only a day, the vines produced lots of them all summer.

When the morning glories wilted in late afternoon, the moonflowers took over.
Their huge, sweetly scented white flowers opened at the end of the day and stayed open all night.

On hot summer nights their tropical fragrance permeated the air and made the front porch
feel rather exotic and mysterious.

To bring more color to the scene, I hung baskets of fuchsias and impatiens
in varied shades of pink among the vines.

The hanging baskets and vines growing around the porch totally transformed the look of the cottage.

They made an ordinary, rather rundown little house look inviting and charming.

Climbing, trailing, and cascading plants add romance to any garden, whether they are grown in pots or in the ground. Vining plants allow gardeners to achieve visual effects that are unattainable with any other type of plant. They have a multiplicity of uses: vines can camouflage eyesores on the property, such as when they tumble over a cinderblock retaining wall; they can decorate a lattice screen, create vertical interest when grown on a trellis, cover a fence, divide space, create welcome shade under an arbor, or ramble about a patch of ground. Vines are at home in gardens of vastly different styles. You can let them romp about in carefree abandon, or carefully clip and train them into formal topiaries.

The goal of this book is to introduce you to a host of climbing, trailing, and cascading plants to grow in your garden to create special effects. You will find a variety of plants discussed—perennials that return year after year, annuals that burst into lavish bloom and disappear at the end of the season, long-stemmed shrubs and woody vines that can become permanent fixtures in the garden, and exotic-looking tropical beauties that thrive in the warmest climates and can in many cases be moved indoors for winter farther north.

The choice of plants covered in this book is eclectic and, I confess, personal. There isn't room in a small book to cover every vine and every plant that will grow in a hanging basket, so my choices began with the plants I like best. But that doesn't mean the book is devoted to plants that grow best on Long Island and in Pennsylvania, where my own gardens have been. I've tried to include some plants of interest for each part of the United States.

The book begins with a look at some of the many things you can do with vines and hanging baskets in your home landscape. Chapter One is full of design ideas—some practical, such as screening a view of the street, some decorative, such as planting a climbing hydrangea to scale the trunk of a large tree. And some of the ideas are just for fun, like adding hanging baskets to decorate a vine-covered arbor.

In order to find the best means of supporting a vine you first need to understand how the vine climbs. Chapter Two explains the different methods vines use to hoist themselves aloft, and which types of supporting structures or devices are most effective for which kinds of vines. There are also descriptions of different kinds of supports for vines, from simple string trellises to arbors and pergolas.

The next two chapters are devoted to planting vines and basket plants, and to caring for plants growing in the ground or in containers. I have emphasized organic methods, because that's how I garden, but more traditional approaches to fertilization and pest control are not overlooked.

Finally, Chapter Five offers descriptions and cultural information on some of the best vines and basket plants for American gardens.

Hardiness I've provided basic information on the hardiness of various perennial plants based on the system of Plant Hardiness Zones developed by the United States Department of Agriculture. This is not a perfect system by any means; for one thing, it cannot take into account local climate variations that can affect plant hardiness. But it is the best system available to us, and it does serve as a useful guide to which plants might or might not be likely to survive in your garden. Most good gardening encyclopedias include a zone map (look for editions that have the most recent version, which was introduced in 1990). You can also buy a copy through the Superintendent of Documents in Washington, D.C. Use hardiness zone listings as a guide, but learn about the growing conditions that exist right in your garden, too. Keeping a garden diary that includes notes on plant performance and observations of weather conditions over a number of years can become the most helpful guide you'll ever have.

Hardiness zones do not really apply to annual plants that live only for one year, but annuals, too, have varying temperature preferences and tolerances. Annuals are usually classified as hardy, half-hardy, or tender. Hardy annuals grow best in cool weather, can tolerate some frost without suffering damage, and their seeds can survive prolonged exposure to cold. You can sow seeds outdoors in fall or plant seeds or plants in early spring when the soil can be worked and the threat of heavy frost is past.

Half-hardy annuals will generally tolerate light frost but cannot stand repeated exposure to below-freezing temperatures. They tend to grow well in cool, moist conditions.

Tender annuals cannot take any frost at all and grow best in warm weather. Do not plant them in the garden until all danger of frost is past in spring.

About Plant Names You will find that I use both botanical and common names for plants thoughout the book. Many gardeners call plants by their common names, which are colorful and familiar, but common names differ from place to place, and many plants have several. It can be confusing. Sometimes the same common name is given to two or more different plants. For example, plants in two different genera—*Jasminum* and *Trachelospermum*—are both called Confederate jasmine or star jasmine.

Botanical names can be confusing, too, especially when botanists change them, as sometimes happens. But they are more widely recognized than common names. Using a plant's botanical name makes it easier to get exactly the plant you want from a nursery, and to find information on a particular plant in this and other gardening books.

So don't be intimidated. And don't worry if you can't pronounce botanical names—few of us are experts in Latin, and you will learn in time. Some books and magazines (such as the American Horticultural Society's *American Horticulturist*) provide pronunciation guides to plant names.

Basically, a plant is identified by two or three names. The first name, which appears in italics beginning with a capital letter, is the genus name. It identifies a group of closely related species to which the plant belongs. Genus names are often descriptive of a plant's appearance, or they may honor the person who first identified or named the group.

A plant's second name, also italicized, denotes its species. A species is a single unique plant, or a group of very closely related plants that are alike except for small variations such as leaf size, flower color, leaf variegation, or plant size. Species names are often descriptive. For instance, a species name of *scandens* is a tipoff that a plant has long climbing or perhaps trailing stems.

The word species is often abbreviated as sp. or, when more than one plant is referred to, spp., in cases where the actual species name of the plant is not given. For example, a group of honeysuckles might be called *Lonicera* spp.

Each of the variants within a species is called a variety or cultivar (short for cultivated variety). A variety develops as a result of a natural mutation, and a cultivar is a variety that develops in cultivation, often as a result of intentional breeding. But the terms are often used informally, with both kinds being referred to as "varieties." In botanical nomenclature, a variety appears third, often preceded by the abbreviation var. in Roman type. A cultivar name is usually given in Roman, beginning with a capital letter and enclosed in single quotation marks.

Botanical names will become more familiar the more you use them, and will soon become second nature to you.

By whatever names you call them, vines can capture your imagination like no other plants in the garden. Their high spirits and exuberant growth will continually surprise you. And hanging baskets let you bring these delightful plants right up to your front door, where you can enjoy them at close range. I hope this book will inspire you to add a few vines and hanging baskets to your garden.

CHAPTER ONE

Designs with Vines

This chapter explores ways to use vines and make them a part of the garden.
Whether you grow them in the ground or in containers,
vines are versatile. In fact, once you include some vines in your garden
you will probably find them indispensable.

Seldom the stars or focal points of the garden, vines play an important supporting role in many successful landscapes. In the right location at a particular time of year, a vine can have its chance to shine, as well. You can choose a flowering perennial vine such as clematis or trumpet creeper (*Campsis radicans*) to bring glorious color to the garden for several weeks in spring or summer, or an annual vine like canary creeper (*Tropaeolum peregrinum*) that will brighten the scene all summer long. Or you might select a climber such as jasmine (*Jasminum spp.*) or moonflower (*Ipomoea alba*) for its enchanting fragrance. Other vines come into their own in autumn; porcelain berry (*Ampelopsis brevipedunculata*) produces astonishing turquoise fruit in September, while the leaves of Virginia creeper (*Parthenocissus quinquefolia*) and Boston ivy (*Parthenocissus tricuspidata*) turn to flame before they drop.

This chapter offers ideas for using vines to good effect in a host of different situations.

Architectural Uses for Vines

Because vines are so strongly linear you can employ them as architectural elements in the garden or landscape. Vines trained on upright supports are an excellent source of vertical line in the garden. Vertical plants can add interesting accents to beds and borders of mostly shorter plants, and they are essential for adding height. A garden planted in a gradation of heights allows all the plants to be seen, and also creates a feeling of depth and greater space in the garden.

Vertical vines can be especially helpful in a landscape that contains no trees. If you have moved into a newly built house on a cleared lot, of course you want to plant some trees right away. But big trees cost many thousands of dollars, and they must be treated with great care during transporting and after the landscape crew has planted them. So most homeowners plant saplings. During the early years while the trees are growing, vines can give you greenery off the ground. They are also, as we will see later, a quick source of welcome summer shade.

Screening Vines planted in a row, as a screen, can provide a green or colorful backdrop for a flower garden, if you don't happen to have a group of large evergreen shrubs or a conveniently located woodland to serve the purpose. And vines are often more appealing than a solid wall or fence behind the garden.

You can use vines as screens to define the boundaries of your property, to define or divide space, to buffer sound, to serve as a windbreak, to create shade, and to block out things you don't want to see.

Vines create a screen that is not solid; you can see through gaps in the foliage to catch glimpses of the area beyond the screen. The permeability of a screen made of vines creates the illusion of greater depth and more space—a trick that is especially effective on a small property, where a solid wall would make the space seem cramped and confined.

Where you put a screen—whether or not you cover it with vines—depends upon the size of the area in which you place it and the distance from which you will view it. If you will be quite close to the screen (seated next to it in a small backyard, for instance), it can be just 5 or 6 feet tall and still serve its purpose. The farther you are from a screen, the taller it must be to work. A screen can be made with deciduous or evergreen vines, both of which have their merits. Evergreen vines are green all year, and some of them offer the bonus of variegated foliage or seasonal blossoms. Deciduous vines afford a greater choice of ornamental qualities: flowers in spring, summer, or fall (or from spring until frost in the case of some annuals), brilliant autumn foliage, or colorful fruit.

You can use vine screens to divide space, separating one part of the garden from another or serving as the "walls" of a garden "room." Trained on a row of freestanding trellises or lattice screens, the vines can provide the effect of a hedge, but the range of choices is far greater. Instead of using a solid wall or a plain high fence to divide space, you can enjoy the textural contrast and color offered by vines. Goldflame honeysuckle (*Lonicera* × *heckrottii*), for instance, sends out clusters of lovely purple-pink flowers with yellow throats all summer. English ivy stays green all year. Trumpet creeper grows thick and leafy, and blooms for a month or more in summer.

Located along a property line, vines trained this way can divide your property from your neighbor's. A divider of vines is friendlier than a wall, more colorful and private than a fence, and less work to maintain than a tall hedge. For a more open type of divider, train vines on a pergola instead of making a screen.

Wisteria covering an arbor and latticework fence screens a view of a nearby highway from this water garden.

Purple and white morning glories and Jack Be Little pumpkins cover a wrought iron fence that divides two neighboring properties.

Installed next to a patio or deck, latticework panels or simple trellises covered with vines can serve as a screen to provide privacy or reduce noise. If you position the vines on the south side of the patio, they will give you shade as well.

Vines trained around a strategically placed arch—whether the arch is freestanding or enclosing a gate in a fence—can also serve a number of architectural purposes. They can frame a favorite view of the garden or of distant scenery, or quietly draw attention to a sundial, birdbath, or other special feature in the garden. Or you can place the arch to highlight a prized plant. The vine-covered arch can provide a charming entry into the garden, or in a large garden it can serve as a transition from one garden area to another.

The best vines to use for screening are twiners such as clematis or honeysuckle, or those with tendrils, depending upon the type of support used. See the list of Vines for Screens for more suggestions.

To maintain a neat, controlled look—which is best for a space divider—choose a vine that takes shearing well (such as ivy) and keep it trimmed. Or plant a vine that is naturally neat of habit and will stay under control without much clipping, such as one or more of the large-flowered clematis hybrids. Climbing roses are classics for training over garden arches, but bear in mind that you will need to fasten the long canes to the arch, and they will need pruning each year.

You might prefer to try out the idea of a vine-bedecked space divider before fully committing yourself, to see if you like the look. A low-risk option is to install supports that are easily removed, such as a wood frame strung with sturdy strings or wires, or covered with plastic garden netting. Plant an annual vine the first year; morning glories (*Ipomoea* spp.), moonflowers, sweet peas (*Lathyrus odoratus*), and scarlet

Morning glories trained over a rustic arbor above a bench create a private retreat in a corner of the garden.

runner bean (*Phaseolus coccineus*) are a few good possibilities. If you like your living wall, next year you can pour cement footings to firmly anchor the supports, and choose a long-lasting material such as rot-resistant cypress or redwood. There are also attractive, durable garden arches made of plastic.

Privacy and Shade Vines are excellent as screens that provide you with privacy and shade. Trained to cover an arbor or gazebo or other enclosed structure, vines create a cool, leafy hideaway where you can sit quietly to read, watch birds, or contemplate the mysteries of life, or where you can enjoy a peaceful family dinner *al fresco* or a romantic picnic for two. A garden seat with an arch above it, all covered with jasmine or grapevines, becomes a lovely spot in which to take a break from gardening chores or survey the glories of the garden, or just delight in the illusion that time has stopped and the rest of the world has gone away.

Place a latticework panel or a freestanding trellis covered with clematis or honeysuckle in front of the seat, and you've got your own private retreat.

Panels of latticework, or trellises installed in a row, to the south of a picnic table can create a cool, leafy, even flowery screen that casts shade in an open, treeless area.

On a series of pergolas or arches over a path, you can use vines to create a leafy tunnel in which to walk. Even a stretch of homely chainlink or mesh fencing can serve as the basis of a leafy screen when covered with vines.

To transform the front porch from a public entry to a shady, private outdoor room, screw cup hooks (the small hooks you would use to hang coffee cups in your kitchen cabinet) into the underside of the porch roof and the top of a wooden railing and run heavy-gauge fishing line or wires vertically between them. Set potted vines at the bottom and let the vines climb the wires to create a living screen. Bright-flowered morning glories or nasturtiums (*Tropaeolum majus*), or fragrant sweet peas or moonflowers are some good choices for screening a porch in this way.

To shade a porch in a more permanent and less enclosing manner you can train vines to grow around the perimeter of the porch roof. The traditional means of support where I grew up in Pennsylvania was to make a frame of lengths of metal pipe that came up on both sides of the porch and horizontally out from the edge of the roof across the front of the porch (and sometimes around the sides as well). This frame was then covered with chicken wire. The vines were planted at the two front corners of the house foundation, and trained to grow up to the porch roof and then across the front of the porch. The vines in effect extended the porch roof horizontally and made the porch shadier.

The extra shade is especially welcome on west-facing porches that are bathed in sun during the afternoon. In hot climates the shade can make the difference between being able to use the porch before dark and being trapped indoors in the air conditioning all day. The shade keeps the house cooler inside, too.

In my hometown, trumpet vine and wisteria were the favorites for shading porches. Dutchman's pipe (*Aristolochia durior*), grapevines, bougainvillea, cup-and-saucer vine (*Cobaea scandens*), and jasmine are other good choices.

In a small city backyard you can make a roof of vines to provide shade where there's no space for trees, and to screen off your garden from the view of upstairs neighbors whose windows look down into your yard. Train the vines on a grid or diamond pattern of plastic-coated wires strung horizontally above the yard or patio to create a rooflike cover. Build a frame of horizontal beams supported by posts around the perimeter of the area you want to cover and string the wires between the beams. You can use narrow wood strips or lattice instead of wires if you prefer, but they will not last as long. Plant vines to climb the posts and spread out over the "roof." Sweet autumn clematis (*Clematis paniculata*) and grapevines (*Vitis spp.*) are both good choices.

This approach is also good in rooftop gardens, so long as the supports—and the plants themselves—are sturdy enough and tightly secured to withstand the strong winds.

Softening Lines A plain masonry wall or an unadorned brick building facade can look rather cold. But vines can soften the severe lines of walls, fences, and buildings, and make them more attractive. Covering the wall of a brick, or stucco house with vines can also lower summer cooling bills. Their shade prevents the masonry from collecting so much heat on sunny summer days.

Vines enhance a building by adding their appealing lines, interesting foliage patterns and textures, and sometimes flowers as well. They offer relief from the harsh simplicity of an empty expanse of brick, stone, or stucco. Vines make chimneys look softer. They can turn a city rooftop into a leafy bower. Vines trailing from windowboxes add charm to the facade of a city brownstone. Vines rambling along the top of a stone retaining wall lend a playful grace that wasn't there before.

Clinging vines are the ones to grow directly on masonry surfaces. Evergreen English ivy is a classic, as is Boston ivy, which loses its leaves in winter but puts on a brilliant show in autumn before baring its stems. The closely related silvervein creeper (*Parthenocissus henryana*), which is suited to mild climates, has pretty leaves with white veining and purple undersides. Creeping fig (*Ficus pumila*), where it is hardy, traces fanciful, deceptively delicate patterns on light-colored stucco or brick (the vines are more tenacious than they look). Climbing hydrangea (*Hydrangea anomala* subsp. *petiolaris*) offers elegant, flat-topped clusters of white flowers in summer. Virginia creeper provides fruit for hungry birds in late summer and autumn.

Clinging vines do not, as a rule, harm solid masonry surfaces. Architects and homeowners debate this point, but the consensus seems to be that if the masonry or the mortar which binds it is old or damaged, the rootlets or other holdfasts by which the vines attach themselves will most likely worsen the problem. But if the brick, stone, stucco, or mortar is sound, vines will probably not break it up. Vines will damage wood surfaces, however, so it is important to prune them to keep them off wood shingles and siding, and away from doors and windowframes.

To enliven a rail or wood-slat fence, or dress up a picket fence, vigorous growers like sweet autumn clematis, anemone clematis (*Clematis montana*), and silverlace vine (*Polygonum aubertii*) are hard to beat.

If your aim is to festoon the front of the house with vines dangling romantically from windowboxes, choose vines that will trail, such as vinca or sweet potato vine (*Ipomoea batatas* 'Blackie'). Trailing vines are also appealing spilling over the sides of large tubs and planter boxes.

A cascade of ivy softens the hard lines of a cement retaining wall, and provides a backdrop for colorful roses.

Fast-growing vines like morning glories can camouflage a shed, lath house, or other outbuilding and make it more attractive.

Camouflage If there's an eyesore on your property that you can't, for one reason or another, get rid of, you can probably cover it up with vines. Vines can hide the compost pile, disguise an old shed, or spruce up the garage. If your garage is located at the end of your backyard, as is the case on so many small, narrow city lots, covering the wall with vines makes the garage seem like part of the garden instead of its abrupt end. That necessary but less-than-aesthetically-pleasing toolshed can look positively charming with morning glories or honeysuckle spilling over it. Just trim the vines or train them to keep them away from the door so you can get in and out easily.

You can use vines to cover a cinderblock retaining wall, too. There are two ways to do it. One is to plant clinging vines at the base of the wall and let them climb it. Or you can plant trailing vines behind the top of the wall and let them dangle over the edge and down the front in a cascade of greenery.

Vines can hide a multitude of sins in the yard. If you are stuck with a utility pole (or its bracing cable) on your property you can make it somewhat less obtrusive by planting vines to climb it. Vines will ramble happily over an old tree stump that's too large and difficult to remove, or a rusty chainlink fence that's still too sturdy to replace. Canary creeper (*Tropaeolum peregrinum*) is wonderful for hiding a chainlink or wire mesh fence, as are morning glories, silverlace vine, and the vigorous clematis species such as anemone and sweet autumn clematis.

The best vines for most kinds of camouflage are those that grow quickly and have large leaves. Dutchman's pipe, hops (*Humulus* spp.), morning glories, and nasturtiums are some good possibilities.

Vines as Decoration

In addition to their practical uses, vines can be purely decorative, too. Vines are so versatile that you could almost consider them the special effects department of the garden. You can do all sorts of tricks with vines. The photographs on these pages should give you some ideas. Look at them, then go outside and look at your house, walk your property. Imagine where you might put a vine or two . . . or ten. You will undoubtedly come up with lots of ideas of your own for interesting ways to use vines in your landscape.

Entries
If your household is like most you probably don't use your front door much to go into and out of your house. Most of us enter by a side or back door. Because we don't use the front door very often, we don't pay much attention to the front of the house or put much effort into making it appealing. As long as the paint's not peeling and the porch light works, we don't think about dressing up the entrance.

Morning glories trained over an arch and along a fence make an inviting entry to this front yard.

But the front door is where you greet visitors and welcome friends and relatives, and a few strategically placed vines can make the entrance prettier and more inviting. The idea is to use just a few vines as decorative accents. You don't want to totally obscure the front of the house; you might like to imagine yourself living in a jungle, but visitors and the mail carrier shouldn't have to beat a path to your door. Dense vegetation is also unwise for security reasons—it is often more enticing to burglars. In the front of the house, a few neatly maintained vines add a dash of color and a bit of whimsy or romance. Lots of vines will only look unkempt.

Here are some suggestions for using vines around the front of the house:

Train vines to climb porch posts and railings. You can let them grow on and weave themselves over, around, and through railings, or simply tumble over the top. Coral vine (*Antigonon leptopus*) is a good plant to festoon a porch rail in a southern location. If a wooden or wrought iron railing edges the steps to the porch you could train a vine to wrap around it.

If the porch is very small, or if you have just a stoop and no real porch at all, a trellised vine along one side of the porch adds a decidedly charming touch as well as a bit of privacy.

If your house has a bare foundation, put a small garden bed in front of it instead of the usual boring foundation shrubbery. Vines on strings or a trellis next to the foundation provide a backdrop for shorter garden plants and visually connect the house to the ground. At the same time, you've hidden the foundation.

Vines are lovely on a lamppost, too, or twining around the post that supports the mailbox. Another way to use vines on a mailbox is to let them dangle over the sides. You can purchase wooden planters that fit over a standard mailbox, with the planting cavity directly above the top of the mailbox. Fill the planter with potting mix and plant small-leaved ivies, variegated vinca, or trailing flowers like lobelia or fuchsias to spill over the edges. Just keep the plants away from the mailbox door by clipping or training them.

Hyacinth bean bedecks a mailbox and its supporting post, combining with black-eyed Susan to add a colorful highlight along the street.

The colorful leaves of kolomikta vine are splashed with pink and cream. Here the vine grows on wire fencing in front of a wall.

Clematis and honeysuckle weave their stems through a latticework fence, and make a lovely combination.

Fences and Walls Wood fences made of rails, pickets, or stakes practically beg for a garnish of vines. Climbing and rambler roses are glorious on rail fences. Jasmines are lovely, too, and the flowers of most species are fragrant. Morning glories and their relatives cypress vine (*Ipomoea quamoclit*) and scarlet starglory (*I. coccinea*) are handsome on fences with slender uprights, although you will need to install strings or vine hooks to help them to the top.

Sweet autumn clematis and silverlace vine will climb and spill practically anywhere, and can turn a fence into living draperies that are spangled with stars (the clematis) or flecked with foam (the silverlace vine) as summer fades into autumn.

Small-leaved vines will trace interesting patterns on a plain wall. A light-colored stucco wall presents a perfect canvas on which vines can sketch their designs. If the vines fill in as the years go by, and the wandering lines become a leafy mass, you can restore the pattern by pruning carefully. Remove some leaves to reveal the line of the stems, and shorten or remove some stems entirely to put some empty space back into the mass and create a new pattern.

Creeping fig and miniature or small-leaved ivies are ideal for decorating a wall in this way. These vines will cling to the wall without assistance. You can make patterns with non-clinging vines as well, by using vine hooks to attach and guide them along the wall. When selecting vines to grow on a wall, consider the size of the leaves in relation to the size of the wall. A miniature-leaved ivy cultivar, or creeping fig, may be too delicate for a large wall. A large-leaved vine on a small wall, however, looks worse.

Another way to decorate a bare wall with vines is to espalier them. Stretch wires across the wall in the pattern you wish to create, attaching them with screw eyes or hooks at either end. Simple parallel horizontal or vertical lines (called cordons in espalier) are easiest to achieve, but you can also try for a grid, a diamond-shaped diagonal grid, a U shape, or some fanciful creation of your own imagining.

When the wires are in place, plant the vine or vines at the base and train the stems on the wires. Prune away all stems that are not part of the design.

A vine espalier will grow more quickly than an espaliered tree and will probably be easier to maintain.

Trellises

Whether you install them in front of a wall or standing on their own in a lawn or garden, trellises can be nearly as good-looking as the vines they support. Trellis-making was an art form in France a couple of centuries ago, and many kinds of trellises are still available. Gardeners handy with hammers, nails, and saws can build their own. Trellises are discussed in more detail in Chapter Two.

The best vines to display on trellises are those which are not dense enough to use for screening or camouflage. Vine and trellis should work together to create their pleasing effect, the softness of leaves, stems, and flowers an appealing counterpoint to the spare geometry of wood or plastic. Most vines that look good on trellises are appropriate for latticework as well. See the list of Vines for Trellises for some suggestions.

Formal Accents

Allowed to go their own way, vines tend to be free spirits. They twine and twirl, dip and curl, send stems looping and arcing off in different directions. Vines are generally best at producing lushly romantic or fun and whimsical effects. But they can also behave quite properly. Careful pruning and training can control the freeranging habit of some vines and turn them into perfectly controlled guests that are welcome at the most formal of landscape parties.

Vines adapt well to simple espalier techniques. In fact, the trellising system preferred for wine grapes—which is designed for productivity rather than aesthetics—looks like the horizontal cordon method of espaliering fruit trees.

Vines for Trellises

The vines listed here will climb a trellis or lattice, but are not dense enough to use for screening.

Bengal clock vine
Black-eyed Susan vine
Canary creeper
Clematis hybrids
Climbing snapdragon
Dicentra scandens
Firecracker vine
Flag-of-Spain
Golden trumpet vine
Honeysuckle
Hyacinth bean
Jasmine
Love-in-a-puff
Mandevilla
Mountain fringe
Porcelain berry
Purple bell vine

Vines for Trees

These vines will climb trees and large shrubs without harming them.

Boston ivy

Canary creeper

Clematis (will need help to climb a tree)

Climbing hydrangea

Dicentra scandens (shrubs only)

Everlasting pea (shrubs only)

Ivy

Japanese hydrangea vine

Nasturtium (shrubs only)

Philodendron

Trumpet creeper (shrubs only)

Virginia creeper

You can also train some woody vines as standards, producing balls of foliage and flowers atop tall, straight stems. A pair of English ivy standards in tubs flanking the front door make for an elegant entrance. Standards can also provide vertical accents in the garden, or take the place of small trees.
The horticulturists at Longwood Gardens in Pennsylvania one recent summer placed standards of golden trumpet vine (*Allamanda cathartica*) in their annual borders, where they looked like small, neat trees covered all summer with huge yellow flowers.

Gardeners in the North who keep tropical vines from year to year by growing them in tubs brought indoors over winter may find standards a good idea. Training the standards requires regular, meticulous pruning, and staking when the vines are young (or permanently if their stems will not grow thick enough to support the ball of topgrowth). But they take up a lot less space than unpruned specimens.

Tree-form standards are the simplest topiary style, but vines with flexible stems can be trained to more elaborate shapes as well. Fast-growing, small-leaved ivies and creeping fig are ideal for training on a wire topiary form, or one filled with moss. You can buy a form or make your own. There are lots of shapes to choose from, from elegant geometric cones and spirals to fanciful animals.

Trees and Shrubs
Vines will decorate other plants as well as structures. Clinging vines such as ivy and climbing hydrangea will scale the trunk of a big old tree. Clematis will lace their stems through the branches of a large shrub or a small tree, and are especially lovely and surprising on evergreens. Sweet autumn clematis will climb a tree trunk, spread out into the branches,

and hang down in great green draperies and ribbons that are covered with starry white flowers at the end of summer. Ivy will provide year-round garb for a tree, but don't use the common, large-leaved English ivy. Instead, opt for a less vigorous, small-leaved cultivar, perhaps a variegated one such as Goldheart, which has golden yellow centers on its green leaves.

Vines can make evergreen trees, shrubs, and even hedges appear to bloom. They can add a second color or an extra season of bloom to deciduous trees and shrubs that produce their own flowers.

You can create marvelous effects by "layering" vines, growing two different vines together. Plant climbing roses and hybrid clematis together, or honeysuckle and roses. Show off the stunning vermilion flowers of Scottish flamethrower (*Tropaeolum speciosum*) or the brilliant yellow blossoms of canary creeper against a backdrop of deep green evergreen English ivy. Let sweet peas or clematis scramble over honeysuckles to have flowers in both spring and summer. Another way to layer vines is to plant a clinging evergreen like euonymus or ivy on a wall, then install a trellis in front of the wall to feature a flowering climber.

Choose carefully when selecting vines to grow on trees and shrubs. While some vines, such as those listed on the opposite page, will not harm the supporting plant, others can be killers. Bittersweet (either the American or oriental species) will wrap its stems around a branch and squeeze tighter and tighter until it strangles the branch. Several years ago, when my husband and I were clearing out an over-grown garden after moving into our house, we uncovered a young hemlock so completely engulfed by bittersweet that we hadn't even known it was there. The bittersweet had wrapped so tightly around the slender trunk that it cut deeply into the wood. We were able to save the tree, but came away with a good lesson about the intractability of this beautifully berried vine.

Climbing hydrangea will cling to a tree trunk for a beautiful effect. A vine of many virtues, it has handsome foliage and lovely summer flowers, and reveals attractive, peeling bark in winter.

Vines as Groundcovers

Some vines make good groundcovers, spreading over the ground to fill space in areas that don't get foot traffic. The best vines to use are clingers or those with a scandent, trailing, or scrambling habit. Such vines are especially nice on a bank or spilling over a retaining wall. If you use clinging vines for groundcover, take note of what's growing nearby. If there is a tree in the vicinity, the groundcover may climb it and maybe swamp it. Either use a less vigorous vine or, if feasible, move the larger plants.

If you want to use a twining vine as a groundcover, spread out the stems over the ground and pin them down with U-shaped lengths of wire to hold them in place.

Vining groundcovers need not be limited to the usual periwinkle (*Vinca* spp.) or ivy (*Hedera* spp.). Clematis is surprising and lovely as a groundcover (not to be walked on, of course), and grapes flow over the ground in rivers of greenery. You can get a similar effect by letting a vine wander over the top of low shrubs instead of planting them directly on the ground. Perhaps a ground-hugging juniper or a patch of heaths or heathers could support a vine in your garden. Nasturtiums are charming clambering over groundcover shrubs.

Problem Solving

Few of us are blessed with the ideal gardening situation. We have more shade than we'd like, or the soil is poor, or there's simply not enough space to grow all the plants we'd like. But every gardening problem has a solution, and vines are great fixers when you use them creatively.

Consider the problem of insufficient space. Vines are great space savers. In a cramped location where there isn't much room for a garden, and no space at all for a tree or large shrub, a vine could be the answer. You can plant a vine in just a few square feet of soil, or in a big tub, and train it to grow flat against a trellis or wall. Woody vines that come back year after year can substitute for a tree or shrub. Draw some of the stems over a three-dimensional arched trellis and your vine becomes a source of shade as well as greenery.

In the vegetable garden you can save space by training vining crops to grow vertically on strings, trellises, or netting. Plant pole beans and peas instead of bush varieties. Train cucumbers, squash, and melons to climb instead of sprawl. If you grow melons and squash, choose small-fruited varieties and use a trellis that is built in a grid pattern. Support each developing fruit with a cloth sling tied to the nearest crossbar so the stem doesn't break from the weight. You can even train indeterminate tomatoes to grow vertically, fastening the stems to the support and pruning to allow just one main stem and several well-spaced side branches.

Poor soil can always be improved with the addition of organic matter, but some locations are simply too difficult to get to on a regular basis. If you have a steep slope or a high bank, you probably won't want to haul wheelbarrows full of compost to it twice a year. And you certainly wouldn't want to try to maintain a lawn there. But bare soil will only erode. Vines can come to the rescue. You can plant tough vines with a sprawling habit in such difficult locations without worrying about mowing, pruning,

Architectural Uses

By placing a group of ba

for privacy, camouflage,

baskets and allow them

and fill them with a sing

of plant in several color

of a color, such as pale

composition, combine

Repeat plants through

The most important th

with fairly large leaves

periwinkle and lobelia,

hybrida). Also look for

Working with C

large basket (see Chap

are mixing plants in or

if you give some thoug

For maximum impact,

that harmonize or cor

than one plant, and yo

the more color it can

Consider the color of

You might be able to

the walls or the roof.

Neutral-colored cont

They are okay against

green containers are

baskets are even bett

the containers disapp

or fertilizing. Many of the honeysuckles make good groundcovers for difficult locations, as do ivies, Carolina jessamine (*Gelsemium sempervirens*), winter jasmine (*Jasminum nudiflorum*), perennial pea, creeper vines, memorial and Lady Banks roses, Cape honeysuckle (*Tecomaria capensis*), Confederate jasmine (*Trachelospermum jasminoides*), periwinkle (*Vinca* spp.), and grapes.

Designing with Baskets

Hanging baskets planted with vines or cascading plants can serve a variety of uses for gardeners. Hanging baskets of impatiens, ivy geraniums (*Pelargonium peltatum*), and fuchsias (*Fuchsia* spp.) are a familiar sight in summer—sometimes too familiar. Still, there are lots of other plants besides these that will thrive in hanging baskets, and even the old stalwarts can gain new appeal when planted in interesting containers or combined with other plants in an attractive way. Here are some suggestions for using hanging baskets effectively.

Entries Like vines planted in the ground, baskets of colorful plants offer a cheerful greeting to visitors. Hang them from a lamppost, suspend them from a porch roof, or group them next to the front door.

Hanging baskets work well in tandem with windowboxes, too. For multi-level interest, try suspending hanging baskets above windowboxes on the railing of a porch or deck. You'll have a lively cascade of color.

Half-baskets, which have one rounded side and one flat side, are designed to be attached to a wall. You can mount them on a front gate or picket fence, on a wooden railing or wall surrounding a porch or deck, or next to or on a door.

Planter boxes on top of [...]
bring the bright colors [...]
lobelia, and geraniums [...]
high off the ground for [...]
surprising effect.

Tendrilled Vines

These vines use tendrils or leaf stalks to grasp a horizontal support.

Canary creeper

Clematis

Dicentra scandens

Gourds

Grapes

Love-in-a-puff

Nasturtium

Purple bell vine

Sweet pea

*Canary creeper (*Tropaeolum peregrinum*), a relative of the nasturtium, is a twining annual vine.*

Twiners
Darwin and his contemporaries observed that in twining vines, the tip of the stem actually moves about in all directions searching for a support to twist itself around. This rotating motion was even given a name—circumnutation.

Most plants twine in a clockwise direction, although some twine counterclockwise. Clockwise twiners include actinidias, Dutchman's pipe (*Aristolochia durior*), bittersweet (*Celsatrus* spp.), hops (*Humulus* spp.), morning glories (*Ipomoea* spp.), woodbine honeysuckle (*Lonicera periclymenum*), and Japanese wisteria (*Wisteria floribunda*).

Some honeysuckles twine in a counterclockwise direction, as does Chinese wisteria (the direction wisteria twines is one way to distinguish the Chinese from the Japanese type when plants are not in bloom).

A particular species of vine will always twine in the same direction, no matter where or under what conditions it is grown. Guiding the shoot tips of a vine toward a support and wrapping them around it in the right direction will help the vine to get established.

Vines that twine are the ones most likely to be problematic in the garden. Some of the most rampant and invasive weeds, such as oriental bittersweet (*Celsatrus orbiculatus*) and Japanese honeysuckle (*Lonicera japonica* 'Halliana'), are twiners. In fact, most twiners are vigorous growers. But as long as you keep an eye on them and prune when necessary to keep them under control, most twiners do not pose problems.

Twining vines need vertical supports on which to climb. They like to rest side shoots on available horizontal braces, but their growth is directed by the main stem, which reaches for the sky. You can grow twiners on vertical strings or wires, or trellises. To support the side branches, give twiners horizontal supports 8 to 12 inches apart in addition to the vertical lines. Twiners will also climb on netting and grid-pattern trellises, by wrapping their stems around the vertical parts of the support. On latticework they will zigzag upward.

If you want to use a twining vine to trim a retaining wall or the side of your house, you can attach one or more sturdy wires to the wall with hooks or screw eyes that will hold the wire a couple of inches out from the surface of the wall. Use galvanized, copper, or plastic-coated wire that will not rust. To prevent the vine from sliding down the wire when it is covered with heavy snow or ice, install a series of horizontal wires about 6 feet apart. The vine will send sideshoots onto these wires that will hold it in place.

Prune the vines to keep them away from window frames, shingles, and rain gutters. If allowed to grow unchecked, the vines will grow into the rain gutters and block them, and will pry loose shingles by worming their way underneath.

One definite benefit of using twining vines on a grid of wires instead of clinging vines to decorate a wall will become apparent when you have to paint or repoint the wall. All you need to do is simply detach the wires—vines and all—and carefully lay them out on the ground. Then be careful not to step on them or crush them under the ladder as you work. When the job is finished, reattach the wires to the wall.

You can also train the vines through vine hooks instead of installing the wires. Vine hooks screw into the wall wherever you need them. They are easier to install and less expensive than a system of wires, but do not allow for an easy way to remove the vines to do maintenance on the wall.

Do not try to grow twining vines on trees and shrubs. They may be able to climb a trunk or branch that is slender enough for their stems to twine around, but they may end up strangling branches.

Tendrilled Vines
The second group of vines uses tendrils or leaf stems to grab hold of a support and wrap around it. Tendrils are special structures that some plants develop to help them climb. Tendrils are modified leaves, branches, or flower stems that can actually "feel;" they begin to curl when they touch a supporting surface. In so-called leaf climbers, vines whose tendrils are modified leaves, leaves or leaflets may become adapted into the slender tendrils (as is the case with peas), or the leafstalk itself may curl around the support when it makes contact (this is how clematis and nasturtiums climb). Some vines, such as gourds (*Cucurbita* spp.), produce tendrils from modified branches. Others, such as grapes (*Vitis* spp.) and passionflowers (*Passiflora* spp.), have tendrils that could have otherwise been flowers or shoots.

Tendrils curl instead of growing straight like stems because their cells grow unevenly. The cells on the outside part of the stem grow faster than those on the inside, causing the stem to curl. The greater the disparity in growth rates between inner cells and outer cells, the tighter the tendril curls.

The coiling action of tendrils pulls the plant's stem toward the support. If a tendril is unable to find a support to clasp once it has formed, it either dangles in midair or dries up and drops off the plant.

Tendrils can most easily grasp a thin horizontal support. Vines that climb by means of tendrils will grow best on a structure that offers horizontal wires, strings, or narrow wood strips for support.

Morning glories and other twiners climb vertical supports, and will also rest side shoots on horizontal supports.

Twining Vines

These vines wrap their stems around a vertical support.

Bittersweet
Canary creeper
Confederate jasmine
Dutchman's pipe
Firecracker vine
Flag-of-Spain
Honeysuckle
Hops
Hyacinth bean
Jasmine
Kiwi, kolomikta vine
Morning glories and relatives
Scarlet runner bean
Wisteria

Grow these vines on a series of horizontal wires, on a trellis or an arbor designed to incorporate horizontal bars, or on netting or a grid of some sort. They will also climb on other plants by wrapping their tendrils around the host plant's slender stems.

Clinging Vines Some vines have developed structures that can grip onto flat surfaces such as walls, rocks, and trees. These structures are usually roots produced along the stems instead of underground. They may be small rootlets, like those of ivy (*Hedera* spp.), or roots modified into tendrils, like those of Virginia creeper (*Parthenocissus quinquefolia*). In some vines little pads form at the tips of the rootlets when they make contact with a surface. The pads secrete a substance that actually glues them fast. When the pads are firmly in place, the root tendrils curl and pull the stem to the support. Virginia creeper offers an excellent example of these adhesive pads. Darwin and his vine-studying colleagues found Viriginia creeper enthralling.

A rough surface is easiest for clinging vines to grip—stucco, brick, stone, and cinderblock are better than smooth plaster. The vines will even shove their rootlets or tendrils into cracks in the wall to get a better grip. If the wall is old and the masonry is crumbly, the vines can cause damage. But a sound, well-built wall should not be harmed.

Clinging vines will also hold on to the rough trunks of trees and shrubs, and the combination of plants can create striking effects in the garden. One of the handsomest vines to grow on a tree is climbing hydrangea (*Hydrangea anomala* subsp. *petiolaris*), or its oriental counterpart, Japanese hydrangea vine (*Schizophragma hydrangeoides*).

Tendrilled vines, such as these sweet peas, wrap their thin tendrils around a slender support.

Clinging vines, especially evergreens, are quite appealing on the walls of buildings, too, and many of them make good groundcovers as well. English ivy (*Hedera helix*), Canary Island ivy (*Hedera canariensis*), and euonymus all have attractive, glossy leaves that can be had in different sizes and variegations. One thing to keep in mind, though, before you transform your house into an ivy-covered cottage is that winter weather can be tough on these vines. The leaves may suffer during cold, windy winter weather as the sun and wind draw moisture from the foliage that the plant cannot replace because roots cannot draw more from the frozen ground.

If you live where winters are cold and there is little protection from the wind, plant evergreen vines on the north or east side of the house or building, where they will receive the least sun.

Clinging vines such as Boston ivy (shown here) fasten themselves to vertical surfaces with adhesive rootlets or pads. Other clinging vines include climbing hydrangea, English ivy, Canary Island ivy, Japanese hydrangea vine, trumpet creeper, Virginia creeper, and wintercreeper or euonymus.

Avoid planting on the south and southwest sides, which are exposed to the most hours of sunlight per day and also get the warmer, drying, afternoon sun.

Clinging vines on the walls of buildings can be pruned imaginatively to create particular effects. For example, to make a low squat building appear higher, prune vines covering the walls into tall, neat, narrow columns of foliage.

Hook Climbers

Not many vines use hooks (thorns) to climb, and those that do can be pretty unpleasant to work around. These plants are most often relegated to use as barriers. Raspberries and other brambles use hooks, as do catclaw vine (*Macfadyena unguis-cati*) and catbrier (*Smilax glauca*). Hook climbers will latch onto other plants when climbing, but they have to be attached to trellises or other structural supports.

Other Climbers

Some plants we consider to be climbers, such as climbing and rambler roses, bougainvillea, and winter jasmine (*Jasminum nudiflorum*), do not actually climb on their own. These plants are called scandent, which means ascending or loosely climbing. They develop long stems (called canes in roses) that grow upward and simply rest on a nearby support. If no support is available, the stems of these plants will flop over to rest on the ground. Other vines are procumbent, meaning that they will not climb at all unless tied to a nearby support.

31

These plants are good choices to plant behind the top of a retaining wall and let spill over. Those with especially showy flowers, like roses, are lovely fanned out on a fence or displayed on a trellis or arch. Just bear in mind that you will have to fasten the stems to the supports in order for the plants to climb. Fasten the stems with plastic ties or soft yarn; do not use metal staples, which quickly constrict the growing stems.

Annual Vines

Annual vines flower for much of the summer, and are hard to beat for quick color. In addition to true annuals, which go through their entire life cycle in a single growing season, there are some tender perennials that bloom in their first year and can be treated as annuals in climates too cold for them to survive in winter.

The morning glory tribe counts among its members a number of vigorous, colorful climbers. There are of course the true morning glories (*Ipomoea nil*, *I. purpurea*, and *I. tricolor*), which bloom in shades of purple, violet, blue, pink, red, and white, with some cultivars striped or bicolored.

The large, pure white, fragrant blossoms of moonflower (*Ipomoea alba*) open at the end of the day to become a luminous presence in the garden at night, hoping to attract a pollinating moth. Like vampires and ghosts, the flowers disappear with the dawn. Three redheads of the clan are the scarlet-flowered cardinal climber (*I.* × *multifida*), scarlet starglory or red morning glory (*I. coccinea*), and cypress vine (*I. quamoclit*). Flag-of-Spain (*Mina lobata*), which has flowers that open red and fade to yellow, is also related.

If you find red flowers appealing, you might also consider growing scarlet runner bean (*Phaseolus coccineus*) or nasturtiums (*Tropaeolum majus*). Be sure to choose an old-fashioned trailing nasturtium variety such as Gleam. Newer compact hybrids lack the vining habit. In addition to red, nasturtiums come in shades of orange, gold, and mahogany, as well as creamy white.

A truly spectacular red-flowered nasturtium relative is the Scottish flamethrower or vermilion nasturtium (*Tropaeolum speciosum*). Alas, it is very persnickety in terms of climate and needs cool, moist summer weather to grow well. But gardeners in the Pacific Northwest can enjoy the flamethrower's rich, glowing ruby red flowers, which are particularly striking against the deep green background of a hedge or evergreen shrub.

A less demanding relative of nasturtium is canary creeper. This vine grows happily wherever summer heat is not too terribly intense. It has attractive, lobed leaves of bluish green, and bright golden yellow flowers with a fringed edge. The flowers suggest a flock of little birds perched amid the foliage.

Gardeners with a passion for purple can plant hyacinth bean (*Dolichos lablab*) and climbing snapdragon (*Asarina antirrhinifolia*).

A charmer that is often available already in bloom at local garden centers is black-eyed Susan vine (*Thunbergia alata*). Its flat-petaled orange, yellow, or ivory-white flowers have dark centers like their name-sake. The related Bengal clock vine (*T. grandiflora*) has lavender-blue blossoms.

Annuals are naturals for hanging baskets. You can enjoy color continuously from early summer to frost with cascading ivy geraniums (*Pelargonium peltatum*), fuchsias (*Fuchsia* × *hybrida*), petunias (*Petunia* × *hybrida* or *P. integrifolia*), lobelia (*Lobelia erinus*), sweet alyssum (*Lobularia maritima*), tuberous begonias (*Begonia* × *tuberhybrida*), and browallia (*Browallia speciosa*).

Probably the best thing about annuals, aside from the fact that they bloom for so long, is that you can plant different ones each year and totally change the look of your garden.

Cypress vine (Ipomoea quamoclit), a morning glory relative, is grown as an annual. Its distinctive leaves and bright red flowers have real presence in the garden.

Types of Supports

There is a certain amount of confusion about the different structures that can be used to support vines. Everyone knows what a wall is, of course, and tree trunks are pretty obvious, too. But what, exactly, is a trellis? And how is a pergola different from an arbor? It is time for some definitions.

Trellises Trellises are simply structures on which climbing plants are supported or displayed. Trellises can be flat or three-dimensional. They can be placed against a wall or fence, or they may be free-standing. The most versatile trellises have the pieces in a grid pattern or some other combination of vertical and horizontal bars. They can support either twining vines, which use the vertical pieces to climb, or tendril climbers, which grasp the horizontal bars.

Trellises are on the market, in finished form or as kits you assemble yourself, in a variety of shapes, patterns, and sizes. You can purchase grid-type trellis panels of different sizes to use singly or combine with other panels in a modular system. Some of the panels include supporting posts topped with decorative

The exquisite moonflower
opens its large, fragrant blossoms
in late afternoon and
flowers throughout the night.

finials. Some are flat across the top; others are arched, or dipped like a swag. Some trellises are collapsible; you can open them up as far as you need to, expanding them as plants grow taller.

Trellises can be made of metal, plastic, or wood. Wood is, to most people, the most aesthetically pleasing material. A wood trellis can be painted or unpainted. Unpainted trellises are less work because you don't have to repaint them. Use rot-resistant wood such as redwood or cedar for an unpainted trellis.

If you plan to grow vines on a trellis next to the wall of a wood-sided or shingled house, attach the trellises to the wall with angle irons so the trellis does not rest on the wall. The space will allow for good air circulation for plants, and will make maintenance easier.

Flat trellises are usually vertical, combining strips of wood in fans, diamonds, or other patterns. But they can also be horizontal, like the trellises used for growing wine grapes; these are made of wooden posts with wires strung between them. Plastic-coated wires are the best kind to use; they will not rust.

Arches are another form of trellis, and they, too, may be either flat or three-dimensional. Arches are most often used over pathways, along the edge of a garden or property line, or to divide or define spaces in the landscape. A well-placed arch can highlight a special feature of the garden or frame a spectacular view. When combined with a gate through a picket fence or hedge, a vine-covered arch makes a decorative entry to the garden, or to the property from the street.

or plastic-coate·

line to connect·

strings or wires

depending on th

slack lines will sa

Arbors and

been popular in

room in fine we

Arbors and perg

actually differen·

and when cover

supports vines. `

off arches. (The

can be formal, c·

made of tree tru

bench or seat bu

A pergola is real

with an arched r

house, an especi

Vines are trainec

Supporting l

You can purchas

that you twist (lc

with them too m

or dark-colored

the surface. Keer

for shady locatio

in the design you

You can place arches—especially the three-dimensional kind—in a row, one after the other, straddling a path to make a covered walkway (which is often called a gallery). Or you can set arches side by side to mark an edge or boundary line. Pull those arches into a circle and you can use them to surround a birdbath, fountain, sundial, or other feature, perhaps in the center of a formal garden.

You can also create reverse (upside down) arches, or festoons. To make a festoon, you install a row of pillars and connect them with a drooping chain. In formal rose gardens, climbers can be trained up the pillars and along the chains. Festoons allow all parts of the plant, not just the uppermost stems, to be completely exposed to the sun. They can take the place of a fence in a formal garden, and in fact were popular in German rose gardens during the 1800s.

You can wrap a pillar (or tree trunk, for that matter) with chicken wire or hardware cloth to make it easier for vines to start climbing it. This is a technique best used only with evergreen vines such as ivy, however, unless you want to spend the winter looking at bare stems on a wire cylinder.

Sometimes a three-dimensional trellis is what you need. A three-dimensional trellis can turn a vine in a large container into a piece of living sculpture. Freestanding trellises can mark corners of the garden or serve as vertical accents amid expanses of lower plants.

Tall obelisks, columns, and pyramids made of trelliswork were often used in Dutch gardens in the 1600s. Later on, the English Victorians made these structures even more elaborate, adding curlicues and fancy geometric patterns. Plants can be trained up the outside of these trellises, or the forms can be set over the plants, which then climb up through the inside.

In Colonial America, kitchen gardeners made simple tripods or teepees of wooden poles lashed together at the top. You can grow beans on teepees and tripods, or hops, or purely decorative twiners such as morning glories. A teepee can be small enough to fit in a pot—just 1 to 2 feet high— or large enough to let a child sit underneath.

Building Your Own Trellises
Simple wooden trellises are not difficult to build at home, if you have the time and are handy with hammer and nails.

You can make a wood trellis from rot-resistant redwood or pressure-treated wood, from bamboo canes, or for a rustic look, from young saplings or slender branches that are flexible and easy to bend.

Wire fencing or a simple grid-like trellis will support either tendrilled vines like these sweet peas, or twiners such as morning glories and scarlet runner beans.

Golden hops tr
of wooden pole
vertical accent.

Fuchsias grow as shrubs in warm climates, but they make lovely annual plants for hanging baskets farther north.

Finally, mulch around the base of the plant, over the entire rootball or an area of 2 to 4 square feet, with 1 to 2 inches of shredded leaves, cocoa bean hulls, or other loose material, to conserve soil moisture and keep the root zone cooler.

Make sure new plants receive plenty of moisture during their first month or so, as they settle into their new location and send new roots out into the soil. If the weather is dry, water as needed to keep the soil evenly moist but not soggy.

Planting in Containers

The techniques for planting pots, tubs, windowboxes, and hanging baskets made of plastic, clay, or ceramic are much the same. Wire baskets require a different method, and this is discussed later in this chapter.

First, choose the container you will use. Chapter Two contains information on different kinds of hanging baskets. Remember, plastic baskets are lightweight and portable, and hold moisture longer than containers made of clay or other porous material. Clay and ceramic containers are heavier (a plus for containers sitting on the ground) and require strong hangers, but many gardeners like the way they look. Tubs, urns, and barrels that sit on the ground can be made of wood, which has an appealing natural look, stone or concrete, which are stable and strong, or clay.

If you are planting a perennial vine, choose a container that is large enough to hold the vine for two or more growing seasons, to save yourself the chore of repotting every year. Don't use clay pots for perennials that will stay outdoors year-round. Clay is likely to crack when soil freezes in winter.

If you are planting in a wooden tub or half-barrel, line the inside with heavy polyethylene sheeting to extend the life of the container. Poke holes in the bottom and sides of the plastic to allow drainage. If you want to put plants in a decorative hanging container made of wood, or a pottery container that has no drainage holes, it's easiest to use the decorative container as a cachepot. Plant the vine in a smaller pot with drainage holes that will fit inside the decorative container.

Potting Mixes
The best potting mix is one that is loose textured, well aerated, and well drained but able to hold enough moisture for roots to absorb.

A good potting mix should contain soil (except in certain cases, that I will discuss in a minute), a lightening agent (usually vermiculite, perlite, or sharp builder's sand), organic matter (peat moss, leaf mold, or compost), and additional nutrients from fertilizers of either natural or manufactured origin. You can use a packaged potting soil or garden soil in your potting mixes. If you use a commercial potting soil, I recommend that you choose a brand that does not contain any fertilizers. The fertilizers that some manufacturers add to potting soil are sometimes too strong for young seedlings and delicate plants. Overfertilizing stimulates plants to grow too fast, which weakens them. If you use garden soil in your containers, you should first pasteurize it by baking it in a low (200° F) oven for half an hour to kill disease organisms and other pathogens that may be present.

Peat-based potting mixes are widely used by home gardeners and professional horticulturists, and with good reason. These mixes are lightweight (an important consideration where hanging baskets are concerned) and porous, with good drainage. When wet, peat-based mixes are also able to retain moisture without becoming soggy and waterlogged. On the down side, these mixes are difficult to moisten when dry, because dry peat actually sheds water.

You can use one of these preblended potting mixes (Pro-Mix is one well-known brand) right from the package if you like. I prefer to add some potting soil to give the medium more body and nutrient value. You could, instead, add some sharp sand to add some weight. You can add some all-purpose organic or slow-release fertilizer to the potting mix to nourish the plants, or you can feed plants during the growing season as directed in Chapter Four.

Soilless potting mixes are useful in certain situations. A soilless mix is generally sterile, and because it contains no nutrients you can rely exclusively on fertilizers to control the amount and kinds of nutrients your plants receive. A sterile growing medium is usually recommended for starting seeds, since young seedlings are easy prey for disease organisms. Soilless mixes may also make sense in muggy, humid climates, where plant diseases (both soilborne and those carried in the air) are common.

Here are a few recipes for making your own potting mixes. One good all-purpose mix consists of one part soil, one part sharp builder's sand, and one part peat moss. Another all-purpose mix contains two parts soil, one part crumbled compost, and one part sand, perlite, or vermiculite. I used to add bonemeal to potting mixes, too, about a tablespoon per quart of mix, but I don't really feel it's worthwhile anymore. The bonemeal available today is so highly processed that it contains practically no nutrient value, and is no longer the valuable soil conditioner it once was.

Hanging Basket Plants

Here are some good plants to grow in hanging baskets.

Black-eyed Susan vine
Browallia
Creeping zinnia
Euonymus
Fuchsia
Ivy
Ivy geranium
Licorice plant
Lobelia
Nasturtium
Petunia
Sweet alyssum
Tuberous begonia
Variegated vinca
Verbena

Use your imagination when planting hanging baskets. Generous containers can hold more than one kind of plant. Wire baskets, especially, lend themselves to mass plantings. Try these combinations:

Geraniums in the top of the basket, petunias around the top edge, and lobelia on the sides.

Geraniums in the top, petunias around the top edge, and ivy and fuchsias in the sides.

Impatiens in the top with lobelia around the top edge and on the sides.

Impatiens in the top, browallia around the top edge, and lobelia on the sides.

You can experiment with different plant combinations and color schemes from year to year. Put the largest, most upright plants in the top of the basket and small trailing or cascading plants in the sides.

A richer potting mix for ferns and other humus-loving plants combines one part soil, two parts compost, and one part sand, perlite, or vermiculite. Finally, if you prefer a soilless mix, combine three parts peat moss with one part sand, perlite, or vermiculite. Unless you are growing acid-loving plants, add about three-fourths cup of ground horticultural or dolomitic limestone to each bushel of the mix to neutralize the acidity of the peat.

How to Plant

If you are planting a vine in a tub or barrel, you should install a support for the plant—a suitably sized trellis, stakes, or a topiary form—before you plant the vine. If the vine you will be planting requires a tall trellis, it would be wise to place the container against a wall and attach the top of the trellis to the wall to keep it upright. You can also train a vine in a container on wires attached to the wall. If you are planting in a basket, it is best to attach the wires or chains to hang the basket after the plant is in place.

A 1- to 2-inch layer of broken pieces of clay pots, gravel, or pebbles in the bottom of the container will help anchor a trellis, and also insures good drainage. Some gardeners prefer to put a layer of filter charcoal (not barbecue briquettes) in the bottom of the pot for drainage and to sweeten the soil.

Fill the container partway with moist potting mix. Set the plant in the container, keeping as much of its soil-ball intact as you can. Position the plant so that it sits at the same depth it was growing previously in the flat, pot, or nursery container. When the depth is correct, fill the rest of the pot with soil mix.

Water to settle the potting mix around the roots, and add additional mix as needed to bring the soil level up to 1 inch from the rim of the pot. Don't fill the pot all the way to the top or it will be difficult to water.

If you are planting several cascading plants together in a hanging basket, position one in the center of the pot and space the others evenly around the rim of the pot so they will spill over the sides.

Always water well after planting. Remove any excess water remaining in saucers or drainage pans underneath pots a half hour after watering.

Be careful when planting baskets not to overplant and stuff them too full of plants. You must allow some room for the young plants to grow to their mature size. The basket will look a little sparse at first, but the plants, especially if they are fast-growing annuals, will soon fill in. Crowded plants will not be able to develop to their full potential, will need constant fertilizing, and will not bloom as lavishly as they should. Weaker plants will be overwhelmed by more aggressive ones, and will eventually die off.

Planting Wire Baskets Wire hanging baskets lined with sphagnum moss allow you to create spectacular effects. You can plant the sides as well as the top of a wire basket to create a ball of flowers and foliage that completely covers the container. Here's how to do it.

First, soak sheets of sphagnum moss in a bucket of water for a few minutes before you use them. Remove a piece of moss from the bucket, squeeze out the excess water, and place it in the bottom of the wire basket. The moss should cover the bottom and just a little of the sides of the basket. If the moss will not stay in place, fasten it to the basket with green florist's wire. Place a couple of handfuls of moist potting mix on top of the moss.

Next, insert two to four small trailing or cascading plants, roots first, through the sides of the basket, so the roots rest on top of the potting mix in the bottom of the basket. Space the plants evenly around the outside of the basket; how many you use will depend upon the size of the basket. Add more potting mix to cover the plant roots.

Then place a strip of sphagnum moss around the inside of the basket, butting its lower edge against the upper edge of the first piece of moss. Wire the moss in place if necessary. Add potting mix up to the top edge of this strip of moss. Then insert plants, spacing them evenly around the basket and placing their roots on top of the potting mix. Add more potting mix to cover the roots.

Repeat the procedure, adding more moss, then more soil, then more plants, and soil to cover, until you reach the upper rim of the basket. End by planting a few bushy, full plants in the top of the basket. Water well when planting is complete.

There are some alternatives to this basic method for planting a wire basket. You could, if you prefer, line the entire basket with moss, fill it with potting mix, and then punch holes in the sides for planting. Or you could line the basket with black polyethylene instead of using sphagnum moss. Cut holes or slits in the plastic through which to plant, and punch in some smaller holes to allow for drainage of excess water. Finally, you could use a sort of hybrid of the two methods, and line the bottom of the basket with plastic to prevent leaks, and line the sides with sphagnum.

Line a wire basket with sheets of damp sphagnum moss or other fibrous material before filling it with potting mix. You can plant just in the top, or along the sides as well.

CHAPTER FOUR

Caring for Vines and Baskets

Although many of the plants described in this book are very undemanding in terms of maintenance,
all of them need a little care to keep them growing well and looking their best.

In addition to regular maintenance such as deadheading, watering, and fertilizing, this chapter also provides guidance on rejuvenating overgrown and neglected vines, and providing winter protection for plants that may need help to survive winter conditions in your garden. Deadheading is simply clipping or picking off faded flowers. It serves two purposes: first, it keeps plants looking neat and well groomed, and second, it encourages some plants—notably annuals—to continue blooming. An annual plant is biologically programmed to grow, flower, produce seeds, and then die, all within the course of a single growing season. When you remove the dead flowers before seeds have a chance to develop, the plant will keep trying to fulfill its destiny by producing more flowers. If you let sweet peas (*Lathyrus odoratus*) form their pods, for example, the plants stop blooming and the vines begin to die. But if you pick off the old flowers before the pods develop, the plants will keep blooming, as long as the weather does not get too hot.

Deadheading

For the most part, the vines worth deadheading are the ones with large, showy flowers, such as climbing roses (*Rosa* hybrids) and hybrid morning glories (*Ipomoea* hybrids). It's not worthwhile trying to deadhead a plant that produces masses of small flowers, like honeysuckle (*Lonicera* spp.) or sweet autumn clematis (*Clematis paniculata*). And you will not want to deadhead plants that produce fruit that is ornamental or attractive to wildlife, such as porcelain berry (*Ampelopsis brevipedunculata*) or bittersweet (*Celastrus* spp.). Sometimes whether or not to deadhead is strictly a matter of personal preference. Do you want to see hips on your roses in fall? Do you like the look of the silky-tailed seedheads produced by clematis? If so, don't deadhead these plants.

When you do deadhead, cut off the flower stem along with the flower; don't just clip off the flower head and leave the bare stem. On some plants, you can look at deadheading as a form of pruning. When deadheading roses, for instance, if you cut back to a leaf that has five leaflets instead of three, you will encourage the plant to produce flowering, rather than strictly vegetative, shoots.

Do Not Deadhead

If you do not clip off the faded flowers, these vines will develop interesting seedpods or berries that are ornamental or attractive to birds:

Bittersweet
Boston ivy
Clematis
Climbing roses
Euonymus
Honeysuckle
Hyacinth bean
Love-in-a-puff
Pepper vine
Porcelain berry
Silvervein creeper
Virginia creeper

Watering

If you have chosen vines carefully, and planted species suited to your climate and growing conditions, those growing in the ground should need little in the way of supplemental watering. You will need to water during extended spells of dry weather, though. There's an old gardeners' rule of thumb that says gardens need an average of an inch of water per week, whether that water comes in the form of rain or from a hose or sprinkler. That maxim makes a useful starting point, but it does not apply to all plants in all gardens. Some plants need more water than others in order to grow well. Plants with deep roots can tolerate more drought than shallow-rooted plants. See Chapter Five for information on the moisture needs of individual plants. Clay soils dry out more slowly than light, sandy soils, and plants growing in them will not need watering as often. When the sun blazes and the mercury soars, soil dries out more quickly than it does under cloudy, humid conditions.

Where a vine is planted can also affect its need for water. A vine planted next to a tree or shrub will be competing with its larger neighbor for moisture and nutrients. It will need to be watered and fertilized more often than a vine growing in open soil. A vine planted right next to a wall may need more watering, too, if the wall blocks some of the rain that falls from reaching the vine. A plant growing in the shade, but not over the root zone of a tree or shrub, will need watering less often than one in full sun.

Climbing roses need regular deadheading, even moisture, and lots of organic matter to thrive. Fasten the canes to their support at intervals as they grow.

Gardeners with loamy soil can plan on watering about once a week during dry spells. If your soil is very sandy, like the soil in my garden, you will have to water annuals and shallow-rooted plants twice or possibly even three times a week during drought. If you find yourself in this situation, get busy working organic matter into the soil to boost its water-holding capacity in future years. If your soil is heavy and full of clay, you will need to water only every ten days to two weeks during prolonged dry spells.

The best advice I could give any gardener is not to slavishly follow rules and guidelines like the ones I just gave you. Use them as a point of reference, but water your plants when they need it. The best way to tell when your garden needs water is not by looking at the calendar or the thermometer. Instead, go out into the garden—or wherever your vines are planted—and poke your finger down into the soil, or dig a small hole with a trowel. When the soil is dry a couple of inches below the surface, it's time to water.

When you do water, take the time to water deeply and thoroughly. Deep watering encourages plants to send their roots deeper into the soil to seek moisture, instead of concentrating their roots closer to the soil surface where they are more vulnerable to hot, dry conditions.

If you will be away for a couple of days, group potted plants under a tree so they don't dry out so quickly. Water well before you leave.

To minimize the amount of moisture lost to evaporation and allow your watering efforts to do the most good, water in the morning or late in the afternoon. If you water late in the day, be sure there are still a few hours of daylight remaining when you finish so the foliage has time to dry before dark. Wet leaves at night are more susceptible to attack from disease organisms. Try to avoid watering during the peak suntanning hours—10 a.m. to 2 p.m.—when the sun is at its hottest.

Watering Containers Plants growing in hanging baskets and other containers need to be watered

more often than plants in the ground, because the smaller volume of soil dries out much more quickly. How often you need to water depends on the weather, the size of the container, and the degree of drought the plants in it can tolerate. Location also makes a difference; containers in the shade will not dry out as fast as containers that are in the sun for most of the day.

The soil in containers dries out most quickly on hot, sunny, windy days. Plants that need even moisture to grow well, such as lobelia, fuchsia, and ivy geranium will need to be watered daily in hot weather. On windy days you may need to water twice. Plants in small pots and baskets may also need watering more than once a day. The larger the container, the less often you'll have to water.

There are a couple of different ways to check when it's time to water plants in hanging baskets and pots. You can poke your finger into the soil as you do in the garden, or you can lift the container. If the pot feels very light, the soil is dry and it's time to water. Try to water before plants wilt; wilting indicates water stress, and can set back plant growth and delay or decrease blooming.

Scarlet runner beans, like other legumes, fix nitrogen in the soil and actually improve its quality.

When you water, soak the soil thoroughly, until excess water seeps from the drainage holes. To make the water move through the potting soil more slowly you can place a layer of sphagnum moss in the bottom of the pot before filling it with soil. Grouping containers together also slows the rate at which they dry out.

If you are going to be away for several days you will need to make arrangements for your hanging baskets and other pots in your absence. The easiest solution is to have a friend or neighbor water them while you're away. You could, instead, move all the containers to a shady spot and set them on the ground. Water them well before you leave, and don't pour off the excess water from the drainage saucers. Another option is to group the containers together and run a cloth wick from each pot to a reservoir of water. Or you could install small drip irrigation lines and attach a timer.

If some of your plants do begin to wilt, here's a good way to revive them. Sink the container in a bucket of water deep enough so the water level is above the rim of the pot. Bubbles will rise to the water surface as water replaces air in the dry potting mix. When the bubbling stops the soil is saturated. Remove the pot from the water and let it drain. Put the plant in a shady spot to let it recover. Unless the wilting was severe enough to cause permanent damage, the plant should be back to normal in a few hours.

To slow the rate at which the potting mix dries out in a large container, you could spread 1 to 2 inches of loose mulch over the soil surface. Use a fine-textured mulch such as cocoa bean hulls or shredded leaves rather than coarse straw or wood chips.

Fertilizing and Soil Care

After your garden has been established for several years your soil should be in good condition if you have been adding organic matter to it each year. To maintain good quality soil, continue to work in a 1-inch layer of compost or other organic material each year or every two years.

Aim for a balance of nutrients in the materials you put into your soil. If you add nothing but livestock manure year after year, the soil may eventually become high in nitrogen and deficient in phosphorus and potassium. Flowering vines could respond by producing lots of leaves but few flowers. If you make compost from a variety of materials you won't have to worry. But if all your organic matter comes from one source, you will almost certainly need to fertilize plants as well, to make sure they get all the nutrients they need.

Most vines do not need a lot of fertilizing. Feed well-established perennial vines once a year, early in the growing season, with a balanced, all-purpose, organic or inorganic slow-release fertilizer. Feed climbing roses when they begin growing in spring, and monthly thereafter. Stop fertilizing six to eight weeks before you expect the first frost, so new growth can harden before winter.

If you prefer to use a fast-acting 5-10-5 or other quick-release formula, apply it according to the directions on the package.

Annual vines growing in the ground will benefit from booster feedings with organic or other slow-release plant foods once or twice more during the growing season. If you are using fast-release granular or liquid fertilizers you can apply them monthly during the growing season.

Fertilizing in Containers Vines and cascading plants growing in hanging baskets and other containers depend on you, the gardener, to fill their nutritional needs. The nutrients available in the small volume of soil or potting mix in a container are quickly exhausted, and you must replenish them to help plants fuel their growth.

Old-fashioned trailing varieties of nasturtiums cascade over slopes and spill from containers. They bloom best in soil that is not too rich.

To maintain healthy soil for perennial vines growing in containers, freshen the soil once a year. Scrape off and remove the top couple of inches of potting mix in the container (be careful not to damage plant roots in the process). Refill the container up to the same level with fresh potting mix. For an added boost, mix some crumbled compost or packaged organic or slow-release nonorganic fertilizer to the new potting mix before you add it to the container.

Smooth the surface of the potting soil, water to settle it around the plant, then check to make sure the soil is at the same level it was before you removed the old soil. Add or subtract soil as needed to reach the correct level.

Annuals and tender perennials that will be in their baskets or pots only for the duration of the growing season respond very well to quick-release fertilizers. Liquid and water-soluble fertilizers are ideal, and can be applied weekly or biweekly throughout the growing season. Follow the package directions regarding the rate and frequency of application.

If you would rather feed your hanging basket plants organically, incorporate a balanced, all-purpose organic plant food into the potting mix before you plant, again according to the manufacturer's directions. Give plants a booster feeding when they become well established, or midway through the growing season.

No matter what kind of fertilizer you use, don't overdo it. More is not necessarily better where fertilizers are concerned. Too much fertilizer can burn plant tissues, and at the very least it will force plants to put out weak, succulent growth that is prone to attack from insects and diseases.

Controlling Pests and Diseases

The best way to fight pests and diseases is to prevent them in the first place, and the best ways to do that are to grow healthy plants and to keep the garden clean. Healthy, well-nourished, well-cared-for plants are less likely to suffer damage from pests and diseases than weak, sickly plants. Following the cultural practices that have been outlined so far in this chapter will take you a long way toward growing healthy plants.

Keeping the garden clean is the other most important preventive measure you can take. Keep the weeds pulled—at least pull them before they go to seed—and clean up dropped leaves and flowers, and other plant debris. Plant trash lying on the ground provides ideal hiding places for insects to lay eggs, and for disease organisms to gain entry into the garden.

Taking a few simple precautions when you work in the garden can also help prevent the spread of disease. Don't work in the garden immediately after rain or watering, when plants are still wet; harmful organisms may be spread in water droplets clinging to leaves. Don't smoke in the garden; if you are a smoker, wash your hands before working in the garden. Tobacco mosaic virus can be spread to potato vine (*Solanum* spp.), petunias, and other susceptible plants from cigarette smoke.

If you notice disease symptoms on your plants, remove the affected plant part or parts right away. If more symptoms develop and the plant is an annual or a small specimen, remove it from the garden and discard it in the trash. Pick up any leaves, flowers, or shoots that fell from the plant into the garden. Do not put any diseased plant material on the compost pile; even a hot pile will not get hot enough to kill all pathogens.

When pruning away diseased plant parts, put the debris in the trash, not on the compost pile. Don't shred diseased branches to use as mulch. Wash your hands when you finish, and sterilize your tools after each cut, or at least when you complete the pruning. Dip the tools in a solution of one part liquid chlorine bleach to nine parts water.

Allow room for air to circulate among and around plants. Don't crowd plants too close together in the garden. Don't plant vines, except for clingers, right against a wall.

Inspect your plants often throughout the growing season, and take measures promptly when you notice symptoms of pests or disease. If you catch problems early they are easier to solve. Look over your plants carefully, checking leaf axils, undersides of leaves, new shoots, and flower buds for signs of insects or their eggs, or disease damage.

The safest approach is to use natural and plant-based controls that break down quickly after you apply them and do not linger in the environment. One of the most useful products I've found is insecticidal soap (from Safer or Ringer). It has proven effective in my garden against small insects such as aphids and whiteflies, and it does not appear to harm bees, butterflies, or birds.

It's a good idea, too, to learn to recognize the beneficial insects in and around your garden so you will know not to destroy them when you see them. Ladybugs (more correctly called ladybird beetles), praying mantids, green lacewings, and other allies prey on pest insects. If you spot them in your garden, leave them alone to do their work, and consider yourself lucky. You can also purchase beneficial insects by mail to release into your garden, although if enough pests are not present to feed them they will quickly move on.

Euonymus is prone to a type of scale insect that can cause serious problems, especially in the Northeast and Midwest. Dormant oil sprays afford the best control.

If Japanese beetles are always a problem for you, you can spread milky spore disease, which comes in powder form, over your lawn to kill the grubs that winter over there. It will take a couple of years before you see results, but you should notice a marked reduction in the beetle population after that. Bag-type pheromone traps can help control adult beetles, but place them some distance away from your garden, or from the plants usually attacked, or the traps will actually lure more beetles to their favorite foods.

Botanical (plant-based) insecticides such as pyrethrum, rotenone, and neem are also available. They are very effective, and break down quickly when exposed to air, light, or water, so they do not linger to pollute the environment. But you should use them as a last resort. Even botanical insecticides are poisons, and they kill beneficial insects as well as pests. Handle these products as cautiously as you would any other insecticide, and be sure to store them properly.

One pest that can be a tremendous problem for certain vines in the midwestern and northeastern part of the country is euonymus scale. These insects were inadvertently introduced into the United States from the Orient in the nineteenth century. In addition to euonymus, they may attack bittersweet, pachysandra, and English ivy, as well as lilacs. Euonymus scale will seriously damage or even kill plants, so you must take measures if it shows up in your garden. The insects settle on plant leaves or stems, and females develop a dark-colored shell—they look like little brown bumps. The males are white and thin. The best way to fight euonymus scale is to spray affected plants with a dormant oil spray (available at garden centers and from mail-order suppliers) in late March or early April, to smother the insects' eggs. Spray with an insecticide ten days to two weeks after applying the dormant oil, then once or twice more ten days to two weeks apart, to kill any adult insects.

Climbing roses need winter protection in northern gardens to help them survive frigid conditions.

Winter Protection

If you are growing vines that are not reliably hardy in your area, protecting them in winter can get them through conditions they would be unlikely to survive on their own. Winter protection is also a good idea for plants within their normal hardiness range that are growing in exposed, windy locations, and for vines in coastal gardens where winter winds carry salt that can turn the leaves brown.

The best approach for seashore gardens and exposed sites is to plant a permanent windbreak some distance from the garden of mixed trees and shrubs that can stand up to the harsh conditions. Locate the windbreak on the side of the garden from which prevailing winter winds blow. Consult your County

Cooperative Extension office or a reliable local nursery or landscape design firm for advice on plants to use for windbreaks in your area.

There are two basic ways to protect plants from winter cold: mulch the roots and wrap the topgrowth. When the soil begins to freeze in late autumn, spread 2 to 4 inches of loose mulch over the root area of the plant. The purpose of the mulch is to keep the ground frozen during winter mild spells so that roots are not heaved out of the ground during alternate periods of freezing and thawing. Check periodically to make sure the mulch is still in place. If you should notice any exposed roots, gently push them back into the ground if you can, and cover with a thick layer of mulch. Roots left exposed to harsh winter winds and cold temperatures are easily killed.

Wrapping the topgrowth of sensitive plants can protect them from windburn and snow and ice damage. To protect a vine on a freestanding trellis, wrap the entire thing loosely with burlap. To protect vines trained as standards, make a cylinder of chicken wire to surround the entire plant. Fill the cylinder with dry leaves or loose straw. Leave the structure in place until the weather begins to moderate in early spring.

Climbing roses also benefit from special winter care in the northern reaches of their hardiness range. You can protect climbing roses by carefully detaching the canes from their support, and laying them out on the ground. Cover the stems with a mound of soil or a thick layer of straw or leaves. Cover loose material with a tarp or lay some boards across the top to keep it from blowing away.

Northern gardeners can grow tender vines such as allamanda in containers, and bring them indoors for winter. These are trained as standards, for a formal look.

Repotting

Perennial vines that spend their lives in containers need to be repotted every three years or so to keep them from becoming potbound. You will need an assistant to help you repot large vines growing in tubs.

First, water until the soil in the pot is thoroughly moistened. Let the excess water drain away. Detach the vine from its supporting trellis or stakes, and carefully remove the supporting structures from the pot.

Now remove the plant from the pot. If the plant and pot are large, lay the container on its side. Tap on the walls of the container to loosen the soilball, and gently slide the plant out of the pot. From this point you need to work as quickly as possible so the roots do not dry out.

Brush off some of the soil to partially uncover the plant's roots. Untangle the larger roots, working carefully so you don't break them, and very gently spread them out.

If you want to keep the plant in the same pot, prune the roots, removing the bottom third of the large roots. Leave smaller, more fibrous roots intact. If you will be moving the plant to a bigger pot, you don't need to prune the roots.

If you put the plant back in the same pot, have your assistant clean it out while you work on the roots. Brush off the soil and soak the pot in warm water. Use a stiff brush or metal sponge to scrub off fertilizer salts crusted around the rim of the pot. Rinse the pot with clear water.

Repot the plant in fresh, moist potting mix, planting at the same depth it had been growing before.

Prune off any dead or damaged stems. If you pruned the roots, cut back the topgrowth by one-third also, to compensate for the smaller root system.

Return the trellis, stakes, or other supports to the pot and reattach the vine. Water well.

Pruning and Training

Unless you are training them as standards or other forms of topiary, vines generally require little pruning. Hanging basket plants seldom need any pruning at all. Still, a little thoughtful pruning when a vine is young can establish for it a sturdy and attractive framework that will guide its future growth. Pruning can also help keep plants vigorous, keep them from running amok and growing where you don't want them, and promote better bloom. And guiding a vine's stems in certain directions can transform it into a decorative living sculpture that traces a lovely pattern on a trellis, screen, or wall. Vines can be trained in unusual or amusing ways, too, to bring a lush cover of greenery and flowers to unexpected places and corners of the garden.

Young Vines
During its first year or two in the ground, a perennial vine benefits from some guidance. Removing weak stems allows sturdier, more vigorous stems to form the basic structure of the plant, which will keep it strong as it grows. Fastening new shoots to the supporting structure to direct their growth will create a pleasing shape for the plant. Instead of having all the stems bunched up, or sticking out at odd angles, you can fan them out and get them going in more or less the same direction.

Vines that grow quickly and vigorously do not respond well to training when they really get growing, as older stems become thicker and less flexible, so your goal is simply to start them off on the right foot in their first year or two. Thereafter you can let them go their own way.

After you plant the young vine, prune away any damaged or dead growth. Eliminate any crossed stems, and thin out dense clusters of stems in the center of the plant, removing the weakest ones.

If you wish to remove a stem entirely, cut it off at the base of the plant. If you wish to shorten a stem to direct growth or encourage stems to branch and grow bushier, cut back to just above a bud or a node. Choose a healthy, firm bud. A node, or dormant bud, appears as a small lump or swelling along the stem or in a leaf axil.

Cut about ⅛ inch above the bud or node, and angle the cut upward from the bud. If you cut too close to the bud you could damage the bud. But if you cut too far away you will leave a stub that could provide an entry point for disease organisms.

The location of the bud directly below the pruning cut determines the direction in which the new shoot will grow. To promote bushier growth on a sparse plant, make the cut above an inward-facing bud, that is, a bud on the inside of the stem. To encourage a more open habit, prune to an outside bud.

After pruning a newly planted vine, tie the young stems to the trellis or other support. Tie loosely, so the stems are held in place but will not be constricted as they grow and thicken. If your vine is planted some distance away from a tree or wall, as explained in Chapter Three, install some twigs or slender stakes on an angle between the vine and the support to guide the young stems toward the support. Tie the young stems to the twigs.

Keep an eye on the vine during its first growing season. Tie the stems every few weeks to train them and encourage them to climb.

To train a twining vine to climb a pillar or post that is freestanding or part of an arbor or pergola, and that is too thick for the vine to wrap itself around, you can nail or screw fishing line or lengths of wire to the post for the stems to grasp. For a vine that uses tendrils to climb, wrap the wires or fishing line horizontally around the post. Attach the wires about 6 to 12 inches apart. You can use the same technique on a fence, too. If the vine you are growing is evergreen you can wrap the pillar with plastic netting or chicken wire for the stems to climb.

Some vines, such as this trumpet creeper (Campsis radicans) can be espaliered on wires to create a formal pattern against a wall. Painstaking pruning is required.

Established Plants Established vines usually need pruning only to remove dead, damaged, or weak growth, and to keep them under control. Some vines have specific pruning requirements which are discussed in Chapter Five. Here are some general guidelines.

The best time to prune a vine depends on when and how it blooms. Vines that bloom on new wood— the current season's growth—should generally be pruned while they are dormant, in late winter or early spring. Many of the plants that bloom on new wood flower in summer, but this is not true in all cases. The best way to tell if a vine blooms on new wood is to examine the stems when they flower. If the flowering stems are slender and flexible, with smooth skin and often a greenish color, the plant is blooming on new wood. These vines can generally tolerate fairly severe pruning. You can cut back the previous year's growth to leave just a few buds on each, to encourage the growth of more lateral shoots and thus, more flowers.

Prune vines that bloom on old wood within a month after they bloom. These plants set next year's flower buds after they recover from this year's flowering, and if you prune too late you will remove some of next year's buds and dilute the display. Many of the vines that flower on old wood bloom in spring and early summer. Some evergreen vines also bloom on old wood. But again, look at the flowering stems to be sure. If they are thicker, less bendable, and have thick, rough bark, the vine is blooming on old wood. Prune by shortening the blooming stems and cutting back to a healthy shoot or bud lower on the stem.

When you give vines their annual pruning, in addition to pruning flowering stems, remove any dead or damaged stems, get rid of weak, spindly stems, and cut out dense, messy, twiggy growth. You can also cut back stems that have grown beyond the space you have allotted for them.

Vines that you grow for their ornamental foliage, such as ivy and creeping fig (*Ficus pumila*), can be pruned in spring when they begin their new season's growth. Cut back stems that have grown out of bounds, and remove dead, damaged, and weak growth. If you are growing vines on the wall of your house, prune them to keep them from growing onto wooden window frames, trim, cornices, and shingles.

If you have to remove a clinging vine from a wall to do maintenance work on the wall, and you break or injure a lot of the vine's stems in the process, it is probably best to cut the vine back close to the ground and let it start over. Most clinging vines can take severe pruning with no problem. Cut back the plants in early spring, so they will have the entire growing season to restart themselves. If you will not be doing the wall work until summer, cut back the vine later in spring, and let it grow across the lawn over the summer. Reattach it to the wall when the work is finished, holding it in place with vine hooks until it takes hold.

Bittersweet has decorative berries in fall, but it is terribly invasive. If you plant it, prune every year to keep the plants in bounds.

Often, vines produce more flowers on lateral stems than on vertical stems. You can bend and fasten some stems to force them into a horizontal position, or cut back vertical stems by as much as one-third of their length to promote the growth of more lateral shoots.

Rejuvenating Old Vines

Sometimes vines get out of hand. When my husband and I moved into our house, we found that bitter-sweet vines had totally overrun a long-neglected garden and were in the process of strangling a young hemlock. We decided to get rid of the bittersweet entirely (no small task), but in many cases an overgrown vine may be worth saving. You can rejuvenate a vine that has been neglected for years by pruning it severely and then giving it some special care.

Many vines are not harmed by cutting them back almost to the ground (see the sidebar, Vines That Tolerate Severe Pruning). One way to restore such a vine is to cut all the stems back to within a foot or two of the ground. Do the pruning in early spring, just as new growth is beginning. If the soil has been neglected along with the vine, and fertility is low, spread and work in a balanced all-purpose fertilizer, either organic or inorganic, according to the directions on the package, to stimulate new growth. Water well, then mulch.

As the new shoots grow, train them as directed on page 62 for young vines. In subsequent years, care for the rejuvenated plant the same as other vines.

If the overgrown vine is in weakened condition because it has been neglected for so long, do the renovation over a three-year period instead of all at once. Each year prune one-third of the oldest stems, cutting them 1 to 2 feet from the ground. You will have to carefully untangle the top parts of the severed stems from the rest of the plant. Also prune away dead, damaged, and weak, spindly stems. With the third year's pruning you will have cut back all the old, overgrown stems, and the vine should be well on its way to a vigorous recovery.

If the vine is overgrown but not in bad shape, cut back individual stems to bring them back within the area in which you want the vine to stay. Use hand pruners for smaller stems and loppers or even a pruning saw for thicker stems. Staggering the lengths of the stems produces the most natural look. If you shear off all the stems at the same height, your vine will look uncomfortably truncated, more like a hedge than a vine.

train them as directed on page 62 for young vines.

Vines That Bloom on Old Wood

Climbing roses, some

Confederate jasmine

Clematis, early-blooming species and hybrids

Climbing hydrangea

Golden trumpet vine

Japanese hydrangea vine

Jasmine

Kiwi, kolomikta vine

Wisteria

Vines That Bloom on New Wood

Bougainvillea

Clematis, late-blooming species and hybrids

Climbing roses, some

Coral vine

Cross vine

Grapes, some species

Honeysuckle

Jasmine, most species

Mandevilla

Passionflower, most species

Silverlace vine

Stephanotis

CHAPTER FIVE

Vines and Basket Plants to Grow

This chapter is a guide to growing vines and cascading plants suited for hanging baskets. The plants are listed in alphabetical order by their genus name.

Immediately beneath the genus name you will find the most frequently used common name for the plant.

Each entry opens with a description of the plant, which includes its full botanical name—genus, species, and, where applicable, variety or cultivar. I have mentioned cultivars with variegated leaves, flowers of different colors, or other noteworthy attributes.

After the description is an assessment of the plant's hardiness. Hardiness zones given for perennials correspond to the USDA Plant Hardiness Zone Map, which is discussed in the Introduction to this book. Annuals are classified as hardy, half-hardy, or tender, and these terms are also defined in the Introduction.

Basic information on the growing conditions and care needed by the plant are provided under Culture. See Chapter Three for explanations of such terms as full sun and partial shade, and for information on what constitutes average soil or moist but well-drained soil.

At the end of each entry you will find suggestions for ways to use the plant in your garden or landscape.

For some large genera that contain more than just a few species that are good garden plants I have included descriptions of a number of the individual species, in addition to an overall profile of the genus as a whole. Look for these expanded descriptions for Clematis, Jasminum (jasmine), and Lonicera (honeysuckle), among others.

In some cases in which individual species and their growing requirements are markedly different from one another, I have provided separate entries, since that seemed the least confusing way to present the information. Look for separate entries on plants in the genera Ipomoea (morning glories and their relatives), Lathyrus (annual and perennial sweet peas), Rosa (climbing rose hybrids and species), and Tropaeolum (nasturtiums and related plants).

The information in this encyclopedia is not exhaustive and does not go into the fine points of the culture of each plant. But it should give you enough information to decide if a particular plant is one you want to grow, and if so, to grow it successfully.

Actinidia

Actinidia deliciosa (formerly classified as *A. chinensis*), is the Chinese gooseberry or kiwifruit seen in grocery stores. It produces broad, oval, dark green leaves about 6 inches across. Clusters of yellow-orange flowers are followed by the fuzzy-skinned, green-fleshed fruit. The kiwifruit grows vigorously within its range, and can reach 30 feet.

Actinidia kolomikta, kolomikta vine, is another species of hardy kiwi, but this one is grown primarily for its colorful foliage. The oval leaves of the male plants are splashed with creamy white and rich pink. The colors may not reach their full intensity until the plant is a few years old. The twining vines bear clusters of small white flowers in late spring and, if both males and females are planted, edible fruit. Like its relatives, it grows quickly, reaching a height of about 15 or 20 feet. If you want the fruit and your growing season is long enough to allow it to ripen, plant both male and female plants, and prune the plants back severely in late winter to encourage the growth of more fruiting spurs.

Hardiness: Kiwifruit is hardy only as far north as zone 8. Kolomikta vine is hardy in zones 4 to 9.
Culture: Both species will grow in full sun or partial shade, in average garden soil. Kolomikta vine can tolerate soil with a high pH. A long, warm growing season is needed for fruit to ripen. Prune plants in early spring to keep them under control and to remove dead or damaged wood.

Uses: Because they grow rapidly, actinidias are good for screening, providing shade, or hiding an unsightly view. Or grow them on a wall or fence. They will climb a trellis, an arbor, wires, or netting, but need assistance when young.

Adlumia
MOUNTAIN FRINGE

Both the foliage and flowers of this unusual plant are decorative. Mountain fringe, climbing fumitory, or Allegheny vine (*Adlumia fungosa*) is a biennial with small, lacy-looking, three-part leaves as delicately textured as fern fronds. It uses its leafstalks to climb. In midsummer the plant puts out drooping clusters of tiny, white to purplish, bell-shaped flowers. Not yet widely available, this vine is worth a try if you find it offered in a catalog or local nursery. It grows quickly but is not a pest. Mountain fringe reaches a height of about 15 feet when mature. Once established, plants may self-sow.

Hardiness: Mountain fringe is hardy in zones 4 to 9.

Culture: Plant adlumia in partial to light shade. A cool, moist spot protected from hot sun and strong wind is ideal. The ideal soil is well drained but moist, and rich in organic matter, with a slightly acid pH, although the plant will tolerate most average garden soils. Mulch in summer to conserve soil moisture and keep the roots cool. Start plants from seed in spring.

Uses: Plant mountain fringe on a trellis situated where the pretty plant will be readily visible.

Porcelain berry (Ampelopsis brevipedunculata)

Akebia

FIVE-LEAF AKEBIA

Akebia quinata, five-leaf akebia (sometimes called chocolate vine) will grow just about anywhere, even in poor soil. That is either a blessing or a curse, depending on your situation. Given any reasonably good soil, akebia often becomes rampant and invasive, difficult to control or eradicate. But in poor soil on a difficult-to-reach slope, it can be useful. If you can keep it in bounds, five-leaf akebia can be charming.

The fine-textured, five-part leaves are rich green, and cast pleasant shade on an arbor in summer; in the warmer parts of the growing range they are evergreen. The vigorous vines can grow to 40 feet long. In spring they produce clusters of small rosy purple flowers with a fragrance like chocolate (vanilla, to some noses). Oval purple or bluish fruits follow; they are edible but the flavor is insipid.

Hardiness: Five-leaf akebia is hardy in zones 4 to 9. It is most invasive in mild climates and the warmer parts of its range.

Culture: In poor soils give the vine full sun to partial shade; in more fertile soils light shade for much of the day is better. Akebia prefers moist, fertile soils but tolerates very alkaline soils as well as those of generally poor quality.

To control akebia you can grow it in the shade, or in poor soil, or in a large tub. A heavy annual pruning will also help.

Uses: Use akebia for screening, shading, or camouflage, supported on a trellis, strings or wires, or an arbor.

Allamanda

GOLDEN TRUMPET VINE

Golden trumpet vine, *Allamanda cathartica*, is a tender perennial with a multiplicity of uses. In a warm climate where it can stay outdoors permanently, golden trumpet vine can reach 40 feet in length. Elsewhere, of course, it will be smaller. The plants have glossy, oblong, evergreen leaves about 6 inches long, in clusters of four. Yellow, trumpet-shaped flowers about 4 inches long bloom in summer. Cultivars include 'Grandiflora', 'Hendersonii', and 'Nobilis'.

Hardiness: Hardy only in zones 10 and 11; elsewhere grow allamanda in a pot and bring it indoors in winter, or purchase a blooming-size plant from a garden center and enjoy it as an annual, for one summer only.

Culture: Allamanda needs full sun, and moist, fertile soil.

Uses: Train allamanda on a trellis, fence, or wall. You can also train it as a standard, to grace a deck or patio, or to serve as a vertical accent in a bed of summer flowers. It looks like a small, exotic, tropical tree when set behind a lush planting of warm-colored annuals and summer bulbs.

When you bring a potted specimen back indoors for winter, examine it carefully for signs of insects or disease. Cut back on water and fertilizer during the winter to allow the plant to rest.

Ampelopsis

Two noteworthy vines belong to this genus: pepper vine and porcelain berry.

Pepper vine, *Ampelopsis arborea*, is a tendrilled vine for mild—but not warm—climates. It climbs by tendrils to 15 feet or higher. Plants have pinnate leaves that turn red in late summer or early autumn, and clusters of small greenish flowers, but their most ornamental feature are berries that begin white, turn a lovely shade of pink, then eventually ripen to dark purple-black. Pepper vine is native to the southeastern United States. It needs winter protection in the northern part of its range, and can be invasive where winters are mild.

Porcelain berry, *Ampelopsis brevipedunculata*, has arguably the most beautiful berries of any vine.

The tendrilled vines grow to 20 feet and bear three-lobed leaves to 5 inches long that turn reddish in fall. The flowers are inconspicuous, but the berrylike fruits, which ripen in late summer or early fall, are stunning. They begin white, then turn pink, lilac, and eventually a bright to deep turquoise blue. Eventually they turn purplish. The problem with porcelain berry is that it can be invasive and difficult to control. Cutting back the vine each year will help keep it in bounds. The cultivar 'Elegans', which has deeply lobed, variegated leaves, is less rampant, and can even be grown in a hanging basket. Its berries change from yellow to shiny turquoise as they ripen.

Hardiness: Pepper vine is hardy in zones 7 to 9, porcelain berry in zones 5 to 9.

Culture: Pepper vine is not fussy about soil and will tolerate dry soil. Plant it in full sun to partial shade. Porcelain berry also grows well in either full sun or partial shade. It tolerates a pH range from mildly acid to quite alkaline, and withstands hot weather and soil of generally poor quality.

Uses: Grow pepper vine along a wall or an arbor or trellis, for screening or quick cover. You can use stems of the berries, especially in their pink stage, in flower arrangements. Porcelain berry is effective on an arbor or climbing a wall, where its berries will be readily visible (you will have to attach it to the wall with vine hooks). Like those of pepper vine, the berried stems make wonderful additions to flower arrangements.

Plant *Ampelopsis brevipedunculata* 'Elegans' in a hanging basket, or train it against a wall or trellis.

Porcelain berry in both its species and cultivar forms is a good choice for a wildlife garden, too—birds love the beautiful berries.

Antigonon
CORAL VINE

Coral vine, *Antigonon leptopus*, is a gorgeous tropical vine for the warmest American climates. It has deep green arrow-shaped to heart-shaped leaves to 3 inches long (evergreen in the warmer parts of its range) and thin as a sheet of paper. Clusters of bright rose-pink flowers with darker pink centers appear in late summer and fall, or almost continuously in congenial conditions. There is also a white-flowered cultivar, 'Album'. In addition to their ornamental features, the plants also produce edible tubers. The vines climb by tendrils, and can reach 30 feet or more in length.

Hardiness: Coral vine cannot tolerate much frost, and is reliably hardy only in zones 9 to 11. With winter protection, however, it may succeed as far north as zone 8. Topgrowth killed by frost grows back quickly in spring.

Culture: Plant coral vine in full sun or partial shade, in moist but well-drained, humusy soil. It's a good choice for desert gardens where supplementary water is available. This vine grows best in warm weather, and is sensitive to cold.

Uses: Coral vine is a fast grower that is a good choice for screening and quick coverage. It is also lovely climbing a tree or shrub, or trained around a porch.

Aristolochia

Two vines worth the gardener's attention belong to this genus. The better known of the two is Dutchman's pipe, *Aristolochia macrophylla* (formerly classified as *A. durior*). A deciduous perennial, Dutchman's pipe has large, dark green kidney-shaped or heart-shaped leaves. The plant gets its common name from the odd spring-blooming flowers, which are greenish brown in color, and curved with a long tube. They were thought to look like a clay pipe. Dutchman's pipe is a fast-growing twiner that can reach 20 or 30 feet.

A similar species for warm climates is California Dutchman's pipe, *A. californica*. Its flowers are smaller, about an inch long, and bloom in early spring before the heart-shaped leaves develop.

A tropical relative of Dutchman's pipe is calico flower, *Aristolochia elegans*, which can be grown in

Coral vine (Antigonon leptopus)

zones 10 and 11. It has triangular leaves, and dark purple flowers spotted with white. Like Dutchman's pipe, the blossoms of calico flower have a long, tubular throat. Although not as bizarre as Dutchman's pipe, the flowers might be better described as curious rather than pretty.

Hardiness: Dutchman's pipe is hardy in zones 4 to 8. California Dutchman's pipe and calico flower are suited to zones 10 and 11.

Culture: Plant Dutchman's pipe (both species) in full sun to light shade, in any reasonably fertile soil. Clay soils suit it just fine.

You can propagate new plants by division, softwood cuttings, root cuttings, or from seeds.

Uses: The broad leaves make Dutchman's pipe excellent for screening, or you can grow it to shade a porch or cover an arbor. It will also thrive trained on a tripod of poles for a vertical accent in the garden. Warm-climate gardeners can grow calico flower for screening or cover.

Asarina

CLIMBING SNAPDRAGON

Asarina antirrhinifolia and *A. barclaiana* are nicknamed climbing snapdragon because their tubular, two-lipped flowers resemble those of snapdragons, to which the genus *Asarina* is related. The blossoms also bear a passing resemblance to violets and browallia. The most common color is purple, but there are also white and rose-pink forms. The flowers are produced from midsummer to fall, on vigorous vines that grow to about 8 feet in one growing season. The triangular, lobed leaves are similar to those of English ivy. The plants are sometimes sold under the name of *Maurandya*.

Hardiness: Asarina is perennial in zones 8 to 11, but it will bloom the first year from seed and makes a good late-season annual farther north.

Culture: Plant asarina in full sun, in well-drained, reasonably fertile soil with a neutral to slightly alkaline pH. Climbing snapdragon also tolerates sandy soil and a high pH. It is vigorous and assertive in warm climates, and likely to self-sow.

To grow the plant as an annual, start seeds early indoors and transplant the seedlings outdoors when all danger of frost is past. In warm climates, sow seeds directly outdoors. Established plants can be propagated from cuttings taken in late winter or early spring. Plants will also bloom in winter in a cool greenhouse.

Uses: Climbing snapdragon is delightful dangling from a hanging basket when it is grown as an annual. If you want to treat it as a perennial, train it to climb a trellis instead. The vine will grow to 10 feet where it is hardy.

Begonia

Tuberous begonias (*Begonia × tuberhybrida*), while not vines, are excellent plants for hanging baskets, and bring a shot of bright color to a shady location. The plants grow from tender bulbs which you can start indoors in early spring.

Tuberous begonias produce large single or double flowers (some with so many petals they resemble roses, camellias or carnations) in both bright and pastel shades of red, pink, orange, salmon, yellow, and white. There are "picotee" varieties with red petals outlined in white, or white or yellow petals edged with red. The deep green leaves are lobed, toothed, and pointed. The hot colors are unusual among shade-tolerant plants; most shade plants bloom in white or pastels.

To grow tuberous begonias in hanging baskets, look for cascading varieties whose stems will arch gracefully over the sides of the container.

Hardiness: Tuberous begonias are tender and cannot tolerate any frost.

Culture: Tuberous begonias like partial to light shade and fertile soil. They grow best in cool, moist summer weather. Do not put plants outside until all danger of frost is past in spring and the weather has warmed.

If you start with tubers, plant them in a moist but well-drained soil mix with the concave side up, in late winter or early spring. The tubers need warm temperatures of at least 75°F, with a bit of a dip at night, in order to sprout. Keep the potting mix evenly moist until the tubers sprout.

When shoots appear, plant the begonias in individual pots of rich, humusy potting mix. One good mixture is two parts each of good garden loam, compost or leaf mold, and sharp builder's sand, and one part dried cow manure. Give the plants plenty of bright light until it is time to transplant them to hanging baskets and move them outdoors.

In fall, dig the tubers before the first frost and store them indoors in a cool, dry place.

Bignonia

CROSS VINE

Cross vine, *Bignonia capreolata*, is native to the southeastern U.S. It gets its name not from its flowers but from its stem; cutting open the stem reveals a cross-shaped cross-section of inner tissue.

The tendrilled vines grow to 40 feet or more where they are hardy, with compound leaves composed of pointed, oval evergreen leaflets about 5 inches long. The leaves turn a purplish color in autumn. In late spring clusters of tubular red-orange flowers appear and practically cover the plants.

Cross vine's natural habitat is along the edges of woods, and it can be found in the wild covering shrubs and small trees.

Hardiness: Gardeners in zones 7 to 11 can grow cross vine, and the roots will survive in zone 6 with winter protection although the topgrowth dies back each year.

Culture: Cross vine blooms most lavishly in full sun, but also tolerates partial shade. It needs moist soil.

Uses: The vines grow quickly, and are a good choice for screening, or to cover a wall. The plants spread by underground runners, so a spot where its roots can be confined is best, especially in southern gardens. Cross vine is, unfortunately, rather difficult to find for sale, but it is well worth searching for.

Bougainvillea

The many *Bougainvillea* hybrids available are splendid plants for the warm climates of the desert Southwest, southern California, and south Florida. The thorny, woody vines grow to 20 feet or so and are cultivated for the colorful papery bracts which surround the inconspicuous flowers. Bracts come in shades of magenta, red, pink, orange, salmon, gold, purple, and white. Some newer cultivars open gold and change to pink as they mature. Red and magenta bougainvilleas are the most rampant growers, and pink and white tend to be the weakest. The orange, salmon, and yellow shades fall somewhere in between. Bougainvillea's oval to elliptical leaves are evergreen.

A related plant, *Bougainvillea glabra* 'Sanderana', which is a bit hardier, grows along the Gulf Coast. It bears red-violet bracts in summer.

Hardiness: Bougainvillea is hardy only in zones 10 and 11. Gardeners farther north can grow it in a pot and move it indoors in winter.

Culture: Bougainvillea needs as much sun as you can give it (except in the desert, where it will take partial shade), and plenty of heat. The leaves may suffer damage in cold weather, but plants bloom on new growth and usually recover quickly. Bougainvillea sometimes blooms best after a dry period. The plants are not fussy about soil, growing happily in any average soil unless it is wet. They are quite drought-tolerant once established, and need only an occasional deep watering.

Prune in late winter to early spring to remove any dead or damaged wood, and to keep plants under control. Otherwise no pruning is necessary. When pruning, cut back sideshoots close to a firm bud, an inch or two from the main stem.

Plant bougainvillea either in the ground or in a container.

Uses: Grow bougainvillea on a porch or arbor, or a sturdy trellis. It can be used as a light screen. Fasten the stems to the supports at intervals; they cannot hold on by themselves. You can also train bougainvillea on a wall with the aid of vine hooks, or let it grow over tall shrubs.

Browallia

Browallia speciosa is related to potatoes, tomatoes, petunias, and nicotiana. It is a tropical perennial grown as an annual in American gardens. The compact, bushy plants grow about a foot tall, with thin, rather drooping stems, lance-shaped leaves and five-petalled flowers of purple, violet, blue, or white, with long tubular throats.

Hardiness: Browallia is a tender plant that grows best in warm weather. It cannot tolerate frost.

Culture: Browallia needs a long, warm growing season to bloom from seed. Start seeds early indoors, or buy nursery plants if you live where the frost-free growing season is short. Give browallia a moist but well-drained, fertile potting medium. If the plants are still blooming when the weather turns cool in fall, bring them indoors.

Uses: When grown in a hanging basket, browallia's slender stems will cascade over the sides. It is also lovely planted on the sides or bottom of a wire basket lined with moss (see Chapter Three for information on making a moss-lined basket).

Campsis
TRUMPET CREEPER

Trumpet creeper, *Campsis radicans*, is a familiar late summer sight across the eastern part of the country. The bright orange and red trumpets can be seen on many fences and porches, and can also be found strung out along roadsides where the vines grow happily over trees and shrubs. A tough, vigorous vine, trumpet creeper has become rampant in parts of the South.

Trumpet creeper is a clinging vine that can grow to 40 feet or more. Its attractive compound

Browallia speciosa

leaves are made up of oval leaflets. From early August to early September, the plants produce scores of funnel-shaped flowers of orange and scarlet in clusters near the ends of the stems. The blossoms attract hummingbirds. The cultivar 'Flava' has orangey yellow blossoms.

Hardiness: Trumpet creeper is hardy in zones 5 to 9.

Culture: Trumpet creeper grows well in full sun or partial shade, in any reasonably fertile soil. It can tolerate fairly heavy clay soils, and withstands some drought when it is well established. To keep the vine under control, you can cut the stems back to the main stem (more like a trunk in older specimens) in early spring.

Uses: Grow the vines around a porch, or let them climb a tree trunk. They can be used for screening, too. But avoid planting trumpet creeper on building walls—they can damage wood trim and dislodge shingles.

Cardiospermum

LOVE-IN-A-PUFF

Some really appealing nicknames have been bestowed on this pretty plant. The dark seeds inspired love-in-a-puff and heart-pea or heart-seed; they have a white, heart-shaped mark at the point where they attach to the pod. In fact, the genus name, *Cardiospermum*, is derived from the Greek words for heart and seed. Another apt name is balloon vine, because the round seed-pods look like green balloons.

Love-in-a-puff can be perennial in southern gardens, but it is often grown as an annual. It has three-part leaves with toothed or deeply cut edges, and clusters of beautifully formed but tiny white flowers. The balloonlike seed-pods follow the blossoms. The vines have tendrils to help them climb, and may reach 10 feet in the course of a summer.

Hardiness: Love-in-a-puff is considered half-hardy. Perennial from zone 7 south, it is grown as an annual farther north.

A large-flowered Clematis *hybrid*

Culture: This vine needs full sun and will thrive in any average garden soil. It is easy to grow from seed, and is best sown directly in the garden. Set plants about a foot apart.

Uses: Love-in-a-puff will climb a trellis, strings or wires, or netting. It will also grow on shrubs. You can use it as a light screen, or display its attractive leaves and interesting seedpods purely as a decorative accent.

Clematis

Clematis are among the most beloved of woody vines, and for good reason. They offer an array of flower sizes, forms, and colors, and blooming times from spring to fall. Most gardeners are familiar with the large-flowered hybrids that bloom in late spring or summer, but there are also lovely species clematis that flower at other times of the year. Some bloom in early summer and again in autumn, some do not come into bloom until autumn, and others bloom off and on through-out the growing season.

Clematis comes in a spectrum of colors that is weighted toward the purple to pink range. There are no real oranges and only a few yellows. But there are a host of colors to choose from: purples range from palest lavender to

rich, deep violet, and there are also several shades of blue; there are pinks from soft blush to bright magenta; vibrant crimson and wine red, and white round out the palette. The flowers may be small, just an inch across, or gargantuan, up to six inches wide. The most common flower shape is flat and disklike with broad petals, but the flowers of some clematis are dangling bells or umbrellas, or upward-facing stars. Some clematis are delightfully fragrant.

All vining clematis are tendrilled and climb by twisting their leaf-stalks around a support. The vines can grow 5 to 20 feet long, depending on the species or variety.

Hardiness: Many clematis are quite hardy, growing as far north as zone 3 and south to zone 8 or 9. Hardiness for particular types is given below with the descriptions.

Culture: Clematis appreciate a fertile, loamy, well-dug soil that is light and well drained. The ideal pH, especially for the hybrids, is neutral to mildly alkaline. Most of them will tolerate heavier clay soils as well.

Clematis like their roots to be cool, and do not, for the most part, take well to dry conditions. A good layer of mulch will help conserve soil moisture and moderate temperatures under-ground. The hybrids, especially,

will appreciate a location where the roots are in shade and the vines receive sun or partial shade. When planting clematis in your garden, set the plants an inch or two deeper than they were growing in their nursery containers.

Uses: Clematis are lovely on a lamppost, trellis, or lattice, or clambering over shrubs or climb-ing trees. They can be planted in the ground, or in a large tub to decorate a patio or porch. Vigorous growers such as sweet autumn clematis are excellent for camouflage; this species will envelop fences and walls in a blanket of greenery that in late August to early September is spangled with fragrant white stars.

Clematis are among the best plants to grow on trees and shrubs. They weave their stems among the branches of the host plant, and decorate it with their blossoms like ornaments on a Christmas tree. A clematis can make an evergreen tree appear to bloom.

To grow clematis on a tree, plant it a foot or two away from the trunk, where it will be easier to dig a hole, and install a slanted pole or bamboo cane to direct the vine to the tree trunk. As when planting near a wall, do not plant clematis on the south side of a tree.

Keep the soil evenly moist for the first few weeks after planting, as the plants settle in. Thereafter, water when the soil dries out an inch below the surface. To encourage bushier growth, cut back the long stems by half their length during their first year in the garden. It takes two or three years for clematis to begin producing its full complement of mature growth; if your plants look a little spindly their first year or two, be patient.

Install the supports when you plant clematis, and begin guiding or attaching the vines to it as soon as they are long enough; the stems are slender and stiff, and likely to break in strong wind if not secured.

Pruning: Mature clematis benefits from regular pruning, but the time and manner of pruning depends upon the flowering habit. Those that bloom on wood formed the previous year (generally blooming in spring or summer) should be pruned, if necessary, shortly after they finish blooming. They usually do not need much in the way of pruning except to remove damaged wood and keep the plants within their allotted space. Prune species and hybrids that bloom on new wood (generally later bloomers that flower in summer or fall) in late winter or very early spring, while the plants are dormant. You can cut these back hard, to just above the lowest set of buds on each stem, close to the base of the plant. If you are not sure about the best time to prune, it is better to err on the side of caution, pruning too lightly rather than too heavily.

Types: Following are descriptions of some noteworthy clematis species, and classification of large-flowered hybrids.

Large-flowered clematis hybrids are often divided into three groups according to their flowering habit.

The Patens Group bloom in spring on old wood. Prune them lightly after they bloom, and only if necessary to keep them under control (or, of course, to remove damaged growth). Cultivars in this group include 'Barbara Dibley', 'Barbara Jackman', 'Bees Jubilee', 'Guiding Star', 'Lasurstern', 'Miss Bateman', 'Mrs. Bush', 'Mrs. George Jackman', 'Mrs. Spencer Castle', and 'President'.

The Florida Group hybrids bloom in summer on old wood. Like Patens hybrids, they need only light pruning, if any. Prune after flowering. 'Belle of Woking', 'Dr. Ruppel', 'Duchess of Edinburgh', 'Elsa Spath', 'Enchantress', 'Nelly Moser', and 'Pink Champagne' belong to this group.

The Jackmannii Group blooms in summer and autumn on new wood. You can prune them all the way back to the ground when they are dormant. These hybrids are more cold-tolerant than the other two groups. Jackmannii hybrids include 'Ascotiensis', 'Blue Gem', 'Comtesse de Bouchard', 'Crimson King', 'Duchess of Albany', 'Elsa Spath', 'Ernest Markham', 'Etoile Violette', 'Fairy Queen', 'Gipsy Queen', 'Hagley', 'Huldine', 'Lady Betty Balfour', 'Little Nell', 'Lord Neville', 'Minuet', 'Mme. Andre', 'Prins Hendrik', 'Ramona', 'Ville de Lyon', 'W. E. Gladstone', and 'William Kennett'.

Clematis apiifolia, October clematis, blooms in fall with clusters of small white flowers. Vines grow 5 to 9 feet, with deciduous, compound leaves composed of three leaflets. Hardy to zone 3, October clematis tolerates dry soil and is a good choice for planting on a slope or bank.

C. armandii, evergreen clematis, is for warm climates—the mildest parts of zone 7 and south. It's a fast grower, reaching 20 feet or more. In spring, star-shaped, fragrant white flowers to 2 ½ inches across contrast beautifully with the leathery dark green leaves. This lush vine will climb trees and trail from the branches, or cover fences and walls. It's also lovely on an arbor. The topgrowth may die back in harsh winters in the northern part of its range, but if pruned back to the ground the plant will usually recover.

Hybrid clematis

C. crispa, curly clematis, is another warm-climate species, suitable for zones 7 to 11. Plants grow to 9 feet, with pinnate leaves composed of pairs of small, oval leaflets. Bell-shaped flowers of pale purple-blue appear in mid to late summer.

C. × jackmannii, Jackman clematis, blooms in midsummer on new wood. Hardy to zone 5, the plants grow to about 10 feet, with pinnate leaves. The large flowers range in color from violet to reddish purple. The cultivar 'Alba' has white flowers, 'Purpurea Superba' is deep violet, and 'Rubra' is red-violet.

Jouin clematis, *C. × jouiniana*, flowers in late summer and early autumn. The vigorous vines can grow to 12 feet or more, and have compound leaves with toothed oval leaflets. The flowers are creamy white when they first open, and turn pale lavender-blue as they age. This species makes a good groundcover.

Anemone clematis, *C. montana*, is an early bloomer, flowering in spring on old wood. Hardy in zones 5 to 7, it grows vigorously to 20 feet or more—the most energetic clematis. It can be rampant but you can prune it way back after it blooms to keep it under control. Anemone clematis has compound leaves composed of three toothed, oval leaflets, and masses of lightly fragrant white flowers that take on a pinkish cast as they age. 'Alba' has white flowers, 'Lilacina' is bluish lilac, 'Perfecta' has large white blossoms, and 'Rosea' is rose-colored. The variety *rubens*, sometimes called pink clematis, has rose to pink flowers and purplish green leaves.

Anemone clematis makes a good screen, and is lovely spilling over a wall or festooning a fence.

Another lovely and luxuriant member of the clan is the sweet autumn clematis, *C. paniculata*. It is one of the great delights of the early fall garden. In early to mid September the plants are covered with masses of small, fragrant, starry white flowers that look like foam from a distance. The enthusiastic vines reach 20 to 30 feet, and have compound leaves made up of three lobed or scalloped leaflets. Hardy in zones 4 to 9, sweet autumn clematis is excellent for screening, covering a fence or retaining wall, or carpeting a hillside. The vines have

escaped from cultivation on eastern Long Island and elsewhere in the east, and can be seen draped over shrubs and dangling in great green veils from the branches of trees. They do not, appear to harm the plants they use for support.

The plants are easy to control with severe pruning while dormant—you can even cut them all the way to the ground.

Golden clematis, *C. tangutica*, is a yellow-flowered species that blooms on new wood through much of the summer, and often again in early fall. It grows to about 8 or 9 feet, with compound leaves composed of oval leaflets. The golden blossoms are shaped like bells, and the fluffy seed-heads that follow are especially decorative. Golden clematis is hardy in zones 5 to 9, and is particularly lovely climbing a tree.

Scarlet clematis, *C. texensis*, is hardy to zone 6 and blooms in late summer or early autumn on new wood. The compact vines grow to about 6 to 8 feet, with pinnate leaves and bell-shaped flowers of scarlet or rose-pink to purple-red. This species can tolerate dry soil, and is a good choice for locations where summer weather is hot and dry.

C. viticella, Italian clematis, grows to 12 feet and blooms over much of the summer. The vines have deciduous compound leaves, and bell-shaped flowers of blue, purple, or red-violet. Cultivars

include 'Alba' and 'Albiflora', with white flowers; 'Caerulea', with blue-violet blossoms; 'Kermesina', which is burgundy; and 'Purpurea', which is red-violet or rose-pink. This species is hardy to zone 4 or 5, and is a good choice for screening, covering a fence, or planting on a slope.

Cobaea

CUP-AND-SAUCER VINE

Cup-and-saucer vine, *Cobaea scandens*, gets its nickname from the structure of its flowers. From midsummer to frost the plant bears cup-shaped purple flowers that are pale green in bud and progress from lavender to violet in color when open. Each flower is backed by a green calyx that forms the "saucer" when its segments spread wide open. The vines have smooth oval leaves and can grow to 25 feet in a summer.

Hardiness: Gardeners in most locations grow cup-and-saucer vine as an annual, but it is perennial in zone 9 and south.

Culture: Plant cup-and-saucer vine in full sun or partial shade. Start seeds indoors in early spring if you are growing the plant as an annual, and transplant the seedlings to the garden when all danger of frost is past. Set the flat seeds on edge when planting them.

Uses: Cup-and-saucer vine will grow happily on a trellis or fence, or you can put it to work to shade a porch, create a screen, or camouflage a shed. It will climb a rough-surfaced wall, such as stucco, without assistance from the gardener.

Dicentra

A vining relative of bleeding heart that is finding its way into the nursery trade is *Dicentra scandens*. The vine climbs by tendrils to a height of 10 to 15 feet. It has attractive compound leaves composed of broadly oval leaflets an inch or so long. In late summer and early autumn there are clusters of yellow flowers shaped like elongated hearts dangling from thin stems.

Hardiness: *Dicentra scandens* is hardy in zones 6 to 9.

Culture: Give the plant a location in partial shade; dappled sunlight for most of the day is ideal. Moist but well-drained, humusy soil with a mildly acid pH will allow *Dicentra scandens* to flourish.

Uses: Grow this vine on a trellis, arbor, or lattice screen, or let it climb the trunk and weave itself through the branches of a small tree or large shrub.

Dolichos
HYACINTH BEAN

Hyacinth bean, *Dolichos lablab* (sometimes listed as *Lablab purpurea*), is a decorative legume that has been grown in gardens since the nineteenth century. The fast-moving twining vines can grow to 15 feet or more in a single growing season. The plants have deep purple-green oval to triangular leaves in groups of three, like other beans. In summer they send out clusters of fragrant, purple, pealike flowers. These are followed by shiny pods of bright reddish purple.

Hardiness: Hyacinth bean is perennial in zones 10 and 11, and grown as an annual everywhere else. It grows best in zone 6 and south.

Culture: Like other beans, sow hyacinth bean directly in the garden, in full sun, in soil that is moist but well-drained and reasonably fertile. Do not plant until all danger of frost is past and the soil is warm; hyacinth beans grow best in hot weather. If you live north of zone 7, start seeds indoors in individual peat pots to get a jump on the growing season, and carefully transplant the seedlings—still in their pots—to the garden when the soil has warmed. Plants self-sow in warm climates.

Uses: Install strings, netting, or a trellis for the beans to climb, or plant them next to an arch or an arbor.

Euonymus
WINTERCREEPER

Wintercreeper, *Euonymus fortunei*, is most familiar as a groundcover, but it will climb when its trailing stems meet a vertical wall or other rough surface. Then it climbs by means of clinging rootlets. Wintercreeper has small, oval, evergreen leaves with scalloped or toothed edges. There are many cultivars, including a number whose leaves are variegated with yellow or white. One of the best known is 'Silver Queen', which has leaves with irregular ivory edgings. 'Gracilis' or 'Silver Edge' also has white or ivory variegation. 'Kewensis' has very small, glossy green leaves. 'Minima' has small leaves and grows just 3 feet tall; it's a good plant to grow against a low wall, or to decorate the base of a sundial or birdbath.

When grown in full sun, wintercreeper will send out horizontal branches after several years of growth, and develops larger, shinier leaves. In this mature phase the plant is sometimes called glossy wintercreeper. Mature plants bloom, too, producing clusters of small greenish white flowers followed by orange or beige berrylike fruits.

If your wintercreeper is growing on a wall, prune the horizontal branches that extend out from the wall, to prevent them from pulling down the plant in strong wind or when laden with snow or ice. Shorten the branches by half their length.

Another trailing species, running euonymus (*E. obovata*), grows just 1½ feet high, with oval to oblong leaves and red berrylike fruits in fall. The leaves, too, turn red in autumn. The trailing stems root where they touch the ground, making the plant an excellent groundcover for a slope.

Hardiness: Wintercreeper is hardy in zones 5 to 9, although it benefits from a good winter mulch in zone 5. Running euonymus is hardy in zones 5 to 7.

Culture: Both species will grow in full sun or partial to light shade, in any decent garden soil. They can tolerate clay soils. Prune plants as needed to keep them in bounds.

Unfortunately, euonymus is prone to euonymus scale, especially in southern locations. Where these insects are a problem they can be quite persistent and difficult to control. Propagate euonymus from cuttings.

Uses: Euonymus is best grown on a wall or tree, or as a groundcover. It can be invasive in warm climates, so give it plenty of room.

*Hyacinth bean (*Dolichos lablab*)*

Ficus
CREEPING FIG

Creeping fig, *Ficus pumila*, is a dainty-looking, small-leaved plant whose thin, clinging stems make interesting patterns on a stucco wall. The leathery, dark green evergreen leaves are heart-shaped when young, become thicker and more oval with age, and grow to about 2 inches long. The stems use rootlets to cling to the surfaces they climb, and may reach 30 feet in length. Creeping fig grows quickly and is tougher than its delicate appearance would indicate. But although the plant grows fast and can cover a large surface area, it is well behaved and not invasive.

Hardiness: This plant is hardy outdoors only in zones 9 to 11, able to withstand only an occasional light frost.

Culture: Creeping fig grows best in light to full shade, in moist but well-drained soil of average fertility. Prune the vines if needed to keep them under contol.

Uses: Plant creeping fig on a north- or east-facing wall where it will be out of direct sun. It is especially nice covering a retaining wall, or a wall enclosing a garden. Its quick growth also makes it useful as a screen.

Fuchsia
FUCHSIA × HYBRIDA

Hybrid fuchsias are actually shrubby perennials that are not frost-hardy, but their gracefully drooping branches make them perfect for hanging baskets in cold-winter climates when young. Most gardeners must grow the plants as annuals.

Fuchsia hybrids have dangling flowers made up of a pendent bell-shaped calyx topped with sepals that spread horizontally. They come in shades of red, pink,

Variegated English ivy (Hedera helix cv.)

and purple, as well as white, and are often bicolored. Many varieties are available, some with slender our double flowers. The long, arching stems have oval leaves, and the blossoms are produced at the tips of the stems.

Hardiness: Warm-climate gardeners, especially along the West Coast, can grow fuchsias as shrubs. They are tender and cannot tolerate frost. Cut them back annually for better bloom.

Culture: Fuchsias bloom all summer and are excellent basket plants for shade. In fact, they may burn in full sun. Put them in a location that receives partial to full shade. The plants need regular, even moisture, and moist but well-drained, humusy soil or potting mix.

Pinch back the stem tips to encourage bushier growth. Feed plants in baskets every few weeks with mild all-purpose liquid fertilizer. Fuchsias are prone to insect problems, so be vigilant and take prompt action if problems appear.

The best way for most of us to have fuchsias is to buy plants at a local garden center and discard the plants at the end of the growing season. If you have a greenhouse, you can take cuttings at the end of the season and root them in the greenhouse to produce next year's plants.

Gelsemium
CAROLINA JESSAMINE

Carolina jessamine or jasmine, *Gelsemium sempervirens*, the state flower of South Carolina, is a twining evergreen seen in many gardens in the Southeast. It is most often grown south of Maryland, but it will survive farther north if protected in winter with a thick layer of mulch. The stems may grow 15 to 20 feet long, with glossy, deep green, evergreen leaves. In winter in mild climates, Carolina jessamine produces clusters of flaring, tubular yellow flowers with a pleasant scent. Farther north plants bloom lavishly in spring, then sporadically through the summer. The cultivar 'Pride of Augusta' has double flowers.

Hardiness: Carolina jessamine is hardy in zones 7 to 9, or in mild locations in zone 6 with winter protection.

Culture: Carolina jessamine is easy to grow in full sun to light shade, in any average garden soil. It appreciates shade or a good layer of mulch over its roots. Water plants deeply during dry weather. Prune plants if needed after they bloom.

Uses: This plant is a good choice for shading a porch, to train on an arbor or let spill over a retaining wall or fence, or to ramble over a slope.

Carolina jessamine is poisonous, however, so think twice before planting it if your household includes small children or inquisitive, plant-munching pets.

Hedera
IVY

English ivy, *Hedera helix*, is among the most widely grown of vines, and has been in cultivation for hundreds of years. It is a tough, low-maintenance groundcover, and an excellent cover for masonry walls. English ivy has a vining habit when young, and becomes shrubbier with age.

English ivy has lobed, dark green, evergreen leaves with a satiny sheen, on stems 20 to 30 feet long. In time it can completely cover a wall. There are many cultivars, some with smaller leaves, some with greater hardiness, others with assorted variegation patterns of light green, white, or golden yellow. For example, 'Baltica' and 'Bulgaria' are especially hardy (to zone 3). 'Pixie' has small leaves with white veins. 'Silverdust' has white-edged leaves. 'Pedata', bird's foot ivy, has lobed leaves that look like their namesake.

Gardeners in warm climates can grow Algerian or Canary Island ivy (*H. canariensis*), which has lobed, oval or heart-shaped leaves up to 6 inches long. Plants can grow to 50 feet or more. There are variegated cultivars, some with attractive dark veins, and varieties with purple-red stems. 'Variegata' has creamy white variegation and 'Aureo-variegata' is variegated with yellow. 'Conglomerata' has small leaves.

Hardiness: English ivy is hardy in zones 5 to 9. Canary Island ivy is often seen in southern California, and is hardy as far north as zone 8 or 9.

Culture: English ivy is virtually foolproof. It grows best in shade, and will tolerate a great deal of it, but it also grows in sun, so long as conditions are not too hot and dry. If you want to grow it on a wall, avoid one that faces south. English ivy is not fussy about soil, and tolerates heavy clay. It can be sheared back without harm to keep it in bounds. Canary Island ivy grows best in shade, although it will take some sun, and prefers a moist, fertile soil rich in organic matter.

If you grow ivy as a groundcover, mow or trim the edges to keep plants from spreading out of bounds.

New plants are easily propagated from cuttings. If you want new English ivy plants to climb, take cuttings from young stems; the plants climb when they are young, but develop a shrubbier habit with age. When English ivy is going to bloom, it sends out stiff branches near the top of its growth. If you take cuttings of these stems the new plants will be shrubs, not vines.

Uses: English ivy is an excellent choice for screening or planting on a difficult slope. It also does extremely well in tough city conditions. Its stems will cling by rootlets to brick, stone, plaster, tree trunks, and other surfaces. There is some debate about whether or not English ivy is harmful to the mortar in brick and stone walls, but the consensus seems to be that it is not. If the mortar is already in poor condition, the ivy will exacerbate the problem, but it is not generally believed to cause damage on its own.

Like English ivy, Canary Island ivy can climb a wall or sprawl as a groundcover. You can even make it look like a hedge by training it over a wire or chainlink fence.

Helichrysum
LICORICE PLANT

Licorice plant, *Helichrysum petiolatum*, is a trailing plant whose fuzzy, gray-green, oval leaves are attractive in hanging baskets, especially when planted with brightly colored flowers. The stems can reach 3 feet in length. *Helichrysum* may produce white flowers where the growing season is long, but it is grown primarily for the foliage. The cultivar 'Limelight' has yellow-green leaves.

Hardiness: Licorice plant is perennial in frost-free climates, but is grown as an annual in most U.S. gardens.

Culture: Give the plant a good all-purpose potting mix and a location in full sun. In mild climates where plants are hardy, pinch back the stems during the growing season to keep the plants under control.

Humulus
HOPS

There are two species of hops—one annual, the other perennial. Japanese hops, *Humulus japonicus*, is the annual. It is a twiner to 25 feet with dark green, deeply lobed leaves and scaly, conelike greenish flowers. The cultivar 'Variegatus' has white-splashed leaves. Japanese hops grows quickly; in fact, it sometimes grows too well. Plants may roam all over the place, and they often self-sow in congenial surroundings. This species can be a nuisance.

The conelike fruits of the perennial species, the common hop (*H. lupulus*), are the commercial source of the hops used to brew beer. Fruits are produced only on female plants. Common hop has broad, lobed leaves. Especially handsome is the cultivar 'Aureus', which has yellow-green leaves.

Hardiness: Japanese hops is a half-hardy annual; it can tolerate some light frost. Common hops is hardy to zones 3 or 4.

Culture: Japanese hops grows well in any average garden soil, in full sun to light shade, and has no problem being confined to a container. Direct-sow when the danger of frost is past in spring, or sow seeds indoors four to six weeks before you expect the last spring frost. Pull self-sown seedlings to keep the plants from spreading.

Common hops, too, grows quickly and tolerates a range of soils, although it does best in moist, fertile ground.

Uses: Either species of hops makes a good screen, or you can support the vines on a trellis or tripod. Its fast growth and large leaves make it an excellent means of hiding eyesores in the landscape. Hops will quickly cover an ugly fence or an old shed, or screen off a view of the compost pile. They also provide good shade when grown on an arbor.

*Morning glories (*Ipomoea purpurea *cv.)*

Hydrangea
CLIMBING HYDRANGEA

Climbing hydrangea (*Hydrangea anomala* subsp. *petiolaris*) is a clinging vine that climbs by means of rootlets. It takes two or three years after planting to get established, and thereafter begins to climb. It may eventually reach 50 to 60 feet in height, but it grows slowly. Climbing hydrangea has dark green, oval leaves and, in summer, large white flat-topped flower clusters similar to those of the lacecap varieties of *Hydrangea macrophylla*. The plant blooms for a month or more. In autumn the leaves drop to reveal the plant's attractive, peeling, reddish brown bark.

Hardiness: Climbing hydrangea is hardy in zones 4 to 7.

Culture: Give the plant full sun to partial shade, and moist but well-drained, fertile soil rich in organic matter. It will tolerate clay soils. Make sure plants get plenty of water during their first two years in the garden.

Uses: Climbing hydrangea is ideal for growing on tree trunks or masonry walls or chimneys.

The plant is sometimes still referred to by its old name, *Hydrangea petiolaris*.

Ipomoea
MOONFLOWER

The magical moonflower (*Ipomoea alba*) is the morning glory's nocturnal counterpart. A twining tender perennial grown as an annual, moonflower has the wide, heart-shaped leaves of a morning glory. The large leaves are attractive in their own right, but the irresistible flowers are the real reason to grow moonflowers. They are large—up to 6 inches across—and pure white, with wide petals and a long, tubular throat. The sweet fragrance is delightful—not cloying or heavy. The flowers open in late afternoon or early evening, remain open all night, and close the next morning.

Moonflowers start blooming in early summer in zone 9 and south; farther north they flower from mid- to late summer until touched by the first frost.

Hardiness: Moonflower is tender and cannot tolerate frost.

Culture: Give moonflower a location in full sun, with light, well-drained but fertile soil. It will tolerate sandy soils. Nick the seeds with a file and soak them in water overnight before planting.

The vines need a long, warm growing season in order to bloom. If you live north of zone 7, start seeds indoors in individual peat pots and carefully transplant the seedlings to the garden when all danger of frost is past and the soil is warm. Gardeners farther south can direct-sow when frost danger is past.

Uses: Moonflower is a good choice for covering a trellis or netting to make a screen, or to hide a chainlink fence. In addition to trellis or netting, moonflowers will climb strings or wires, or will trail when planted in a hanging basket. Keep them close to the house or a deck or patio you use frequently, so you can enjoy the scent on warm evenings.

Ipomoea
SWEET POTATO VINE

This interesting foliage plant, which goes by the botanical name of *Ipomoea batatas* 'Blackie', is appearing in some garden centers and nurseries. A tender annual, sweet potato vine has dark purple leaves that are deeply lobed, with the lobes splayed out from a central point.

The plant cascades, rather than climbs, and is a good candidate for a hanging basket. The trailing stems grow 6 to 10 feet long.

Hardiness: Sweet potato vine is tender and needs warm temperatures to grow well.

Culture: Plant sweet potato vine in full sun to partial shade, in a well-drained all-pupose potting mix. Do not put the plant outdoors until all danger of frost is past in spring.

Ipomoea
SCARLET STARGLORY

This morning glory relative, *Ipomoea coccinea*, is also called crimson or red morning glory, an apt description of its flowers. The small, funnel-shaped, bright red flowers with a yellow throat open in the morning. The twining annual vines grow to about 10 feet and bloom for most of the summer. Plants bear large, heart-shaped leaves that can be 6 inches long. In parts of the South scarlet starglory has escaped from cultivation and taken up residence in fields and waste places.

Hardiness: Scarlet starglory is tender and cannot tolerate frost. It needs warm weather to grow well.

Culture: Plant scarlet starglory in full sun in light, fertile, well-drained, even sandy, soil. Like other members of the morning glory clan it cannot tolerate cold; direct-sow when all danger of frost is past and the soil has warmed in spring. Nick the hard seedcoat with a file and soak the seeds in water overnight before planting.

Uses: Grow scarlet starglory in a hanging basket, or plant it to climb a trellis, an arbor, netting, strings, or wires.

Ipomoea
CARDINAL CLIMBER

A vigorous twining annual to 10 feet long, cardinal climber (*Ipomoea × multifida*) has handsome, deeply cut, broadly arrow-shaped fernlike leaves that grow about 4 inches across. Its bright crimson flowers are tubular like those of other morning glories, but the blossoms are pentagonal when seen face-on. They are produced through much of the summer. The flowers are smaller than those of true morning glories, and they have a white eye. Hummingbirds are attracted to them.

Hardiness: Cardinal climber is tender and cannot tolerate frost. It grows best in warm weather.

Culture: Give the plant a location in full sun, and soil that is light and porous, fertile, and well drained. It grows well in sandy soils. Sow seeds directly in the garden after all danger of frost is past

and the soil has warmed in spring. Soak the seeds in water for several hours or overnight before planting.

Uses: Cardinal climber is a good choice for a hanging basket, or you can grow it on a trellis, an arbor, netting, strings, or wires.

Ipomoea
MORNING GLORY

Three closely related species— *Ipomoea nil, I. purpurea,* and *I. tricolor*—are all called morning glories. They are twining annual or tender perennial vines to 8 or 10 feet long, with heart-shaped leaves from 4 to 6 inches across. They are grown as annuals.

The flowers are funnel-shaped, with wide, fluted petals; some *I. nil* cultivars have fringed edges or double petals. The flowers of *I. tricolor* have a white to pale yellow throat. The color range includes white, pink, purple, violet, blue, and crimson. Although each blossom lasts just a single day, opening with the rising sun and closing in the afternoon, the plants produce lots of them right up until frost.

Cultivars of *I. nil* include a large-flowered group known as Imperial Japanese morning glories, and 'Scarlet O'Hara', which has red flowers and white-variegated leaves. Bred from *I. purpurea* are 'Alba', which has white flowers, 'Madame Anne',

whose white blossoms carry red stripes, and the double purple-flowered 'Violacea'. *I. tricolor* has given rise to the perfectly named 'Heavenly Blue', whose breathtaking blossoms are exactly the color of a clear autumn sky, the pure white 'Pearly Gates', 'Blue Star', which has light blue flowers with a darker blue stripe, lavender-pink 'Wedding Bells', and magenta 'Crimson Rambler'.

Hardiness: Morning glories are tender, tolerating no frost and growing best in warm weather.

Culture: Plant morning glories in full sun, in light, well-drained, even sandy, soil. Give *I. nil* and *I. tricolor* fertile soil rich in organic matter. For *I. purpurea*, soil of average fertility is adequate; the plants can self-sow and become pests. Sow seeds directly in the garden after all danger of frost is past and the soil has warmed in spring. Soak the seeds in water overnight before planting.

Uses: Morning glories are delightful twining around a mailbox or lamppost. They will happily climb strings, a trellis, netting, or latticework, or clamber over a fence. They are lovely covering a garden arch or decorating a porch, and make a pretty backdrop for the garden. Or grow them on a tripod or teepee of bamboo canes for a freestanding vertical accent. You can grow morning glories in hanging baskets, too.

Ipomoea
CYPRESS VINE

Sometimes still listed as Quamoclit pennata, cypress vine (*Ipomoea quamoclit*) is distinguished by its delicate, feathery leaves that grow about 3 inches long and are deeply cut into thin segments, somewhat resembling fern fronds. The annual twining vines reach about 20 feet in length. Star-shaped, bright scarlet flowers about $1\frac{1}{2}$ inches long with tubular throats bloom in mid summer.

Hardiness: Cypress vine is tender, tolerating no frost and growing best in warm weather.

Culture: Plant cypress vine in a sunny location, in light, fertile soil that is moist but well drained. Direct-sow when the danger of a late spring frost is past and the soil is warm. Nick the seeds with a file or soak them in water overnight before planting.

Uses: Cypress vine is a good choice to display on a trellis. It will also cover a chainlink fence or climb strings or wires.

Cypress vine (Ipomoea quamoclit)

Star jasmine (Jasminum nitidum)

Jasminum
JASMINE

Jasmines are valued for their star-shaped tubular flowers and glossy evergreen leaves. Many—though not all—jasmine flowers are richly fragrant, and the scent intensifies at night. Jasmine blossoms have been used in perfumes for centuries. Some jasmines are shrubby in habit, and others are twining vines.

Spanish jasmine (*Jasminum grandiflorum*) is a climber with pairs of oval leaves on arching branches and very fragrant white flowers in summer and autumn. The blossoms have been used in perfumery. Plants grow about 4 feet high.

Star jasmine or Confederate jasmine (*J. nitidum*, not to be confused with *Trachelospermum*, which has the same common names) grows 10 to 20 feet long, with narrow oval leaves to 3 inches in length. Its reddish to purple buds open into fragrant white flowers.

Winter jasmine (*J. nudiflorum*) is the hardiest of the jasmines. A shrub rather than a vine, its long, arching stems grow to 10 or 15 feet and root where they touch the ground. To train winter jasmine to a support its stems must be fastened to the support—they will not grasp it on their own. In winter or very early spring the plant produces loads of cheery yellow, unscented flowers. Winter jasmine is a good plant to let sprawl over a hillside or bank.

Poet's jasmine or common jasmine (*J. officinale*) climbs to 20 feet or more, with pairs of dark green, semievergreen, oval leaves. Its clusters of fragrant white flowers, produced from early summer to autumn, are used in perfumery. The forma *affine* has larger flowers than the species and the cultivar 'Aureo-variegatum' has variegated leaves. Poet's jasmine is hardy from the mildest parts of zone 7 southward; it is cultivated outdoors as far north as North Carolina. Plants need no pruning unless you want to use them as shrubs.

Jasminum polyanthum is a shrub reaching 15 feet or more, with narrow, dark green leaves that may be deciduous or evergreen. The fragrant flowers are pink outside and white inside, and produced in clusters from late summer to winter.

Arabian jasmine (*J. sambac*) has been grown in gardens for over a thousand years. The vine has glossy oval leaves to 3 inches long, and clusters of fragrant white flowers that are used to flavor jasmine tea. 'Grand Duke of Tuscany' has double flowers. Although it will only survive outdoors in frost-free climates, gardeners in other places can grow Arabian jasmine in pots brought indoors for winter.

Hardiness: Spanish jasmine is hardy in zones 10 and 11, and often in zone 9 if protected from frost. Winter jasmine survives outdoors as far north as zone 6 if grown in a protected location, and grows south to zone 9. Poet's jasmine is hardy from zone 8 southward; it is cultivated outdoors as far north as North Carolina. *Jasminum polyanthum* grows best in zones 9 and 10. Arabian jasmine is hardy outdoors only in zones 10 and 11.

Culture: All the jasmines will grow in full sun to partial shade, in soil that is reasonably fertile, well drained, and not allowed to dry out. Poet's jasmine and *Jasminum polyanthum* tolerate alkaline soil. Prune plants that need it after they bloom.

Uses: Be sure to plant fragrant jasmines next to your porch or patio, or just outside a frequently open door or window, so you can enjoy the heavenly scent when the plants are in bloom.

Lantana

Lantanas (*Lantana* spp.) are shrubby plants that are grown outdoors in warm climates—sometimes as groundcovers—and as annuals or greenhouse plants where winters are cold. They make good hanging basket plants for sunny locations.

Weeping lantana (*Lantana montevidensis*) is a trailing plant or low, mat-forming shrub with stems to 3 feet long. It has serrated oval leaves that smell rather unpleasant when crushed, and 1- to 2-inch-wide clusters of small, rose-purple flowers in summer and off and on all year.

Yellow sage (*L. camara*) is an upright plant that grows to 4 feet tall. Its rough-textured oval leaves have an unpleasant smell when crushed, but the flowers are delightful. They come in rounded clusters 1 to 2 inches across, with individual flowers starting yellow when they first open, then changing to orange, lavender, or pink. A cluster may contain all four colors at once. Numerous cultivars have been developed, including a white one, 'Alba'.

Hardiness: Weeping lantana is hardy outdoors only in zones 10 and 11. Yellow sage is hardy to zone 8. Farther north, grow the plants as annuals or bring them indoors over winter.

Culture: Both species grow best in warm weather and like plenty of sun. Where winters are cold, start seeds indoors in late winter—February is a good time. The seeds germinate very slowly, so be patient; it can take up to two months. Keep the planting medium evenly moist during this time. Transplant outdoors after all danger of frost is past in spring. Gardeners in warm climates can sow seeds directly outdoors.

Give lantana average garden soil or a well-drained all-purpose potting mix.

Lantanas are easily propagated from softwood cuttings. If you live where the plants are not winter-hardy and you have a greenhouse or very sunny window, try taking cuttings in early- to midsummer to start new plants for next year's garden.

Lathyrus
SWEET PEA

One of the best things for me about moving to a seashore town is being able to grow sweet peas (*Lathyrus odoratus*). I never had any luck with them in Pennsylvania, where the clay soil defied early planting and summer came too soon for the young plants. But on coastal Long Island I've had sweet peas in my garden every year.

These wonderfully fragrant flowers have long been a popular part of flower arrangements, and white ones have figured into many bridal bouquets. Related to edible garden peas, sweet peas grow on tendrilled vines that climb to a height of about 8 feet. There are now also dwarf varieties growing just 2 feet tall. The vines have pairs of oval to rounded leaves that clasp the stem. The flowers resemble those of edible peas or beans and come in shades of red, pink, salmon, lavender, purple, and white. The degree of fragrance varies, with some varieties—particularly older ones—and some colors (notably purple) having the strongest scent. The fragrance of sweet peas is honey-sweet, with a hint of vanilla. 'Antique Fantasy Mixed', 'Old Spice', and 'Painted Lady' are among the most fragrant cultivars.

Sweet peas grow best in cool weather, with temperatures below 75° F. They are thus difficult to grow in places where summer weather comes early and hot. In northern and cool coastal gardens sweet peas may bloom all summer (as they sometimes do in mine); elsewhere they fatigue when the weather turns hot. Old-fashioned varieties tend to hold up better than modern ones in summer. The pods of sweet peas are not edible.

Gardeners in warm climates can plant sweet peas as winter flowers.

Hardiness: Sweet peas are hardy annuals; they can tolerate some frost and grow best in cool weather.

Culture: To grow sweet peas for summer flowers, plant them as soon as the soil can be worked in spring, the same time you plant edible peas. They need plenty of sun, and rich, humusy soil that is evenly moist. It is a good idea in northern gardens to prepare the soil in fall and cover it with a good layer of mulch over the winter. Where spring comes late, start seeds indoors in individual peat pots, and move plants outdoors, planting pots and all, when the danger of heavy frost is past. Gardeners in the middle tier of states can also plant sweet peas in fall, before the soil freezes but late enough in the season that the seeds will not germinate until early spring.

If you are planting in front of a masonry wall, avoid one that faces south, where the heat could easily be too much for the plants.

A time-honored method of planting sweet peas is to dig a trench a foot to 18 inches deep and fill it to 6 inches deep with a mix of good garden soil, crumbled compost or well-composed manure, and sharp builder's sand in equal parts. Plant seeds or transplants in peat pots. As the plants grow, add more of the planting mix over a period of weeks until the trench is full. Then mulch with a couple of inches of shredded leaves.

Lantana camara *cv.*

Soaking seeds in water for a couple of days before planting helps speed germination. Do not soak seeds before planting in fall.

When the plants bloom, pick the flowers regularly to keep the plants producing more. When the hairy pods develop the plants stop flowering. Providing a good layer of mulch and lots of water during spells of hot, dry weather will also extend the flowering time.

Uses: Grow sweet peas on a trellis, strings or wires, netting, or latticework. Or plant them to twine around a mailbox pole or lamppost. Another interesting effect is to allow the vines to climb the branches of a shrub.

Sweet alyssum (Lobularia maritima)

Lathyrus
PERENNIAL PEAS

Two species of ornamental peas are perennial rather than annual—the everlasting pea (*Lathyrus grandiflorus*) and the perennial pea (*L. latifolius*).

Everlasting pea is a tendrilled twiner growing to about 6 feet. Its slightly fragrant purple-pink flowers resemble those of other legumes and appear in early summer, usually in pairs or groups of three. Pairs of oval leaflets clasp the stems.

Perennial pea is a more vigorous vine, also tendrilled, that grows to 9 feet. It has pairs of oval leaflets along the stem, and rose-pink flowers in early summer. There is a white-flowered cultivar, 'Alba', and another, 'Splendens', that has bicolored red and purple blossoms. 'Pink Pearl' has large rose-pink blooms. Both species form pods that are not edible.

Hardiness: Everlasting pea is hardy to zone 6, perennial pea to zone 4.

Culture: Everlasting pea grows best in full sun, with regular moisture. Plant it in moist but well-drained soil rich in organic matter. Perennial pea tolerates a range of soils, including clay. Neither species is fussy about pH, except for very acid conditions, and both tolerate soil well into the alkaline range. Soaking seeds overnight before planting is helpful.

Uses: Grow everlasting pea on a trellis, netting, or latticework, or let it climb over shrubs. Perennial pea tends to grow rampantly, and is a good choice to plant on a bank or slope.

Lobelia

The annual edging lobelia (*Lobelia erinus*) is charming spilling over the side of a hanging basket or planted along the sides or bottom of a moss-lined basket. The compact plants grow just 4 to 6 inches high and have small oval leaves with scalloped edges. Throughout the summer they produce small, dainty blossoms of deep violet-blue, clear sky blue, red, pink, or white. The colored flowers often have a contrasting white eye (center).

Hardiness: Lobelia is a hardy annual and grows best in cool weather.

Culture: Lobelia likes full sun to partial shade, with afternoon shade being especially helpful in warm locations. Give it a fertile, humusy, moist but well-drained potting mix. Never let lobelia dry out—it needs constant, even moisture, but not soggy conditions.

Plant lobelia outdoors when the danger of heavy frost is past in spring. To get an early start, start seeds indoors eight to ten weeks before the average last frost date for your area. Seeds are slow to germinate, so be patient.

The plants may stop blooming and die back in hot weather. If this happens to your plants, shear them back and continue to keep the soil moist. The plants will usually send out new growth and resume flowering later in the season, when temperatures begin to cool off at night.

Lobularia
SWEET ALYSSUM

Honey-scented sweet alyssum (*Lobularia maritima*) is a small, delicate-textured plant that can go into the ground early in spring—ahead of most other annuals. Throughout the summer the plants are covered with tiny white, lavender, purple, or pink flowers.

When planted in the ground, sweet alyssum forms a low, spreading mat of flowers and small light green leaves. Planted near the edge of a container it will spill happily over the side.

Hardiness: Sweet alyssum is a hardy annual. It grows best in cool weather and can go outdoors with lettuce and parsley, when the danger of heavy frost is past in spring.

Culture: Sweet alyssum is easy to grow and undemanding about its surroundings. It will take to any average, well-drained garden soil or all-purpose potting mix, and will tolerate a fair degree of drought once established. It prefers full sun but also grows well in partial shade.

The plants may slow down their blooming and even die back a bit during an extended spell of hot midsummer weather. Shear them back, give them regular watering and a dose of fertilizer to rejuvenate them, and sweet alyssum will go on blooming right into autumn.

Warm-climate gardeners can plant sweet alyssum in fall for winter flowers.

Uses: Sweet alyssum makes a delightful edging for hanging baskets, windowboxes, and gardens.

Lonicera

HONEYSUCKLE

Honeysuckles are a group of vines and shrubs with trumpet-shaped or two-lipped flowers in white, yellow, orange, pink, or red. They can be lovely covering a fence or rambling about a hillside, and some offer the bonus of sweet fragrance in their flowers. All honeysuckles belong to the genus *Lonicera*. As a group they are easy to grow and need little in the way of maintenance. Where space is limited, prune to control growth. Some honeysuckles, however, grow too well and can easily become invasive pests. Chief among these is Japanese or Hall's honeysuckle, *Lonicera japonica* 'Halliana', which is problematic in the eastern and southern United States. This one is recommended only for the most difficult conditions, such as an arid garden with poor soil where little else will grow.

Hardiness: Honeysuckles vary in hardiness, but no matter where in the United States you live, there is probably a honeysuckle that will grow well in your climate. Hardiness of different species is given below with the individual descriptions.

Culture: Most honeysuckles thrive in full sun, although a few, as noted below, tolerate or prefer some shade. They take to a range of soils, but prefer good drainage.

Prune the plants when young to encourage them to branch. Prune mature specimens after they finish blooming to keep them under control and to remove dead and damaged growth. Honeysuckles will bloom perfectly well without pruning, but they tend to grow into dense thickets of tangled stems that only bloom at the ends. Pruning keeps the plants neater. One approach is to cut away all the dead old growth from underneath the younger stems with a hedge clippers. For seriously overgrown plants, cut all the stems back to a foot or two from the ground in early spring. As the new shoots grow, keep them untangled and prune to create a pleasing structure.

Uses: The flowers of honeysuckles are their chief ornamental asset. The showier members of the clan are quite lovely displayed on a trellis or latticework. Others are good choices for covering a bank or slope.

Several of the best vining honeysuckles are described below.

Yellow honeysuckle (*Lonicera flava*), a native of the Southeast, is a twining vine with elliptical leaves, and clusters of fragrant, orangey yellow flowers in late spring to early summer. Red berries follow later in the season. Plants grow to about 12 feet, are hardy in zones 5 to 8, and will tolerate partial to light shade.

Everblooming honeysuckle (*L. × heckrottii* 'Goldflame') is another beauty. Its lovely flowers begin as carmine-red buds that open into fragrant blossoms that are yellow inside and rose-red on the outside. The flowers gradually fade to pink as they age. Everblooming honeysuckle flowers profusely in early summer, and continues sporadically into fall. Red fruits follow in autumn. This species, too, twines and climbs, reaching about 15 feet in height. It is hardy to zone 4 or 5, and grows well in full sun to partial shade. A similar, hardier, but non-fragrant variety is the hybrid *L. ×* 'Dropmore Scarlet', which has bright coral-red blossoms from early to late summer. It grows as far north as Minnesota.

Woodbine (*L. periclymenum*) is an old-fashioned honeysuckle with oval to oblong leaves and clusters of fragrant ivory-colored flowers in early to late summer. These are followed by red berries. The twining vines can grow to 20 feet and are hardy to zone 5. Woodbine can tolerate some shade. The cultivar 'Aurea' has leaves variegated with yellow. 'Belgica' is shrubbier in habit, blooms early, and has fragrant flowers that are purplish on the outside and yellow inside. 'Serotina', a climber seen in English cottage gardens, blooms later, producing fragrant flowers that are purple-red outside and cream-colored inside. 'Berries Jubilee' has yellow flowers.

Everblooming honeysuckle (Lonicera × heckrottii 'Goldflame')

Trumpet honeysuckle (*L. sempervirens*), native to the eastern U.S., is a twiner that's good for screening. Its stems can grow from 10 to 50 feet long, but are typically about 12 to 15 feet. They are dressed in oval to oblong leaves that are evergreen in southern gardens. From late spring to late summer the plant sends forth clusters of trumpet-shaped orange, scarlet, or yellow flowers. The flowers are not fragrant, but they do attract hummingbirds. Trumpet honeysuckle is hardy in zones 4 to 9, and can tolerate partial shade. A number of cultivars are available. 'Magnifica' blooms late. 'Sulphurea' has yellow flowers, 'Magnifica' and 'Superba' have scarlet flowers, and those of 'Cedar Lane' are dark red.

Mandevilla

A lovely vine, *Mandevilla × amabilis* is hardy only in frost-free climates. But gardeners farther north can buy a blooming plant in a container at a local nursery and display it for the summer. You can bring it indoors over winter and move it back out in spring when the weather turns warm.

Mandevilla is a twiner growing to 20 feet, with glossy, evergreen, oblong, ribbed leaves to 8 inches long. Its large, trumpet-shaped flowers, which are produced in clusters almost continuously in warm weather, are pale pink when they first open and gradually deepen to rose-pink. The most commonly grown cultivar, 'Alice du Pont', has bright rose-pink flowers with a darker pink throat.

A related species, Chilean jasmine (*Mandevilla laxa* or *M. suaveolens*) also twines and grows to about 20 feet. It has oval to heart-shaped green leaves, and in summer bears clusters of sweetly fragrant, trumpet-shaped white to ivory flowers about 2 inches across. The blossoms are said to smell something like gardenias.

A similar plant, *Mandevilla sanderi* 'Red Riding Hood', has deep rose-pink flowers with yellow throats, and shorter stems that grow just 6 to 8 feet long. Leaves are oval but smaller than those of *M. amabilis*. The plant will climb or trail.

Hardiness: *Mandevilla × amabilis* and *M. sanderi* 'Red Riding Hood' are hardy outdoors only in zones 10 and 11. Chilean jasmine grows in zones 8 and south. Topgrowth may die back in zone 8 but will regrow in spring.

Culture: Mandevilla grows best in light, well-drained but humusy soil. If you are growing it in a container, plant it in a large tub, in a mix of equal parts good garden loam, peat moss or crumbled compost, and sharp builder's sand. Fertilize every few weeks in summer with quick-release fertilizer, or apply a slow-release formula in early summer and again in midsummer.

Give the plant full sun to partial shade in the North; it needs partial to light shade in warmer climates. The plant rests in winter and drops many of its leaves. If you have a potted plant that's indoors for winter, cut back the stems, do not fertilize until spring, and water only enough to keep the soil from totally drying out.

Prune plants if necessary to keep them under control—they will bloom lustily on new growth. In early spring you can cut back last year's stems to two or three buds.

Uses: Display *Mandevilla × amabilis* or Chilean jasmine on a trellis where their flowers can be appreciated. 'Red Riding Hood' will grow in a hanging basket. If you live where the vine is hardy, it will ramble over a fence or wall.

Mina

FLAG-OF-SPAIN

Also known as crimson starglory, *Mina lobata* is a twining tender perennial vine that grows to 10 or 20 feet. It belongs to the morning glory family, Convolvulaceae. The vines have large leaves with three lobes. In summer the plant bears sprays of irregularly shaped tubular flowers about 3 inches long. They are red in bud and when first open, then slowly fade to yellow as they age. The color change takes place over a period of weeks. Plants in bloom show flowers in red, orange, and yellow all at once; often a cluster may contain all the colors in a vertical progression up the spike, like a row of tiny flags. As you might guess, the changing red and yellow flower color inspired the plant's common name— the Spanish flag is red and yellow striped.

Hardiness: Flag-of-Spain is tender and cannot tolerate frost. It is generally grown as an annual except in the frost-free gardens of zones 10 and 11, where the plant is perennial.

Culture: Plant flag-of-Spain in full sun, in soil that is light-textured, fertile, and well drained. You can start seeds indoors in peat pots in early spring, and carefully transplant the seedlings, pot and all, out to the garden after all danger of frost is past.

Uses: Support the vines on a trellis, strings, or wires.

Parthenocissus

CREEPER VINES

Virginia creeper (*Parthenocissus quinquefolia*), an American native, is a common sight in wooded areas and forest edges in the eastern U.S. A clinging vine that climbs to 30 feet or more by grabbing onto a vertical surface with small adhesive disks at the ends of rootlets, Virginia creeper has compound leaves composed of five toothed, oval leaflets radiating from a central point. In autumn the leaves turn fiery scarlet or red. The small flowers are not very noticeable, but in late summer the vines produce dark blue-black berries when grown in a sufficiently sunny location. Birds love to eat the berries, and are a major means of distributing the seeds and spreading the plants in the wild.

Several cultivars are available, including 'Engelmannii', which has smaller leaves, and 'Hirsuta', whose leaves are hairy on the underside.

A less common relative is silver-vein creeper, *Parthenocissus henryana*. This species is also a clinging vine, but is less hardy. Its pretty compound leaves are composed of green oval leaflets with a white vein and purple underside. The plant produces clusters of inconspicuous greenish white flowers and, in fall, blue-black berries attractive to birds.

Hardiness: Virginia creeper is hardy in zones 3 to 9. Silvervein creeper is suited to zones 7 to 9.

Culture: Creeper vines will grow in sun or shade, tolerating nearly full shade. The fall color of Virginia creeper is brightest when the plant grows in full sun, but silvervein creeper develops its best color in partial shade. In fact, this species can grow in full shade as long as it is not too dense. Both vines do well in dry, even sandy, soil of average fertility, but will grow in poorer soils, too. Set plants close together if you want to cover a wall—they are not bushy.

Uses: Grow either of these creeper vines on walls, fences, or arbors, let them climb a tree trunk, or plant them as ground-covers on a hillside.

Parthenocissus
BOSTON IVY

Boston ivy (*Parthenocissus tricuspidata*) really has nothing to do with Boston except that it used to grow on the walls of many buildings there. It is also seen on buildings of the Ivy League universities. The clinging vines can grow to 50 feet, and the lobed leaves may reach 8 inches in length. In time the vines can completely cover a brick or stone wall. The foliage, which looks similar to maple leaves, turns deep red in autumn. There are inconspicuous small flowers

followed in late summer by blue-black berries attractive to birds.

Numerous cultivars are available, including 'Lowii' and 'Veitchii', whose small leaves are purplish when young, and 'Minutifolia', which also has small leaves. 'Purpurea' has dark purple leaves, and 'Robusta' is exceptionally vigorous.

Hardiness: Boston ivy is hardy in zones 3 to 8.

Culture: Boston ivy grows well in sun or shade, and tolerates dry soils and those with a high pH.

Uses: This vine loves to climb the brick or stone walls of buildings, and will cover windows and all if you let it. A north or east wall is best. Besides buildings, it will also climb tree trunks, arbors, trellises, or retaining walls. In addition to growing it on walls, you can use Boston ivy for screening or cam-ouflage. It is a tough vine that tolerates urban settings and other difficult situations quite well.

Passiflora
PASSIONFLOWER

Passionflowers (*Passiflora* spp.) are a group of tropical or sub-tropical vines, many of which have exotically beautiful flowers and some of which also offer edible fruit. The flowers are intricately structured, with wide petals and a "crown" of filaments in the center of the blossom. The flower structure was thought to contain symbols of the passion of Christ,

which inspired the name passion-flower. Although most of the passionflowers are suited only to the warmest American climates, a few are hardy farther north.

Hardiness: Hardiness of several different passionflower species is given with the descriptions below.

Culture: Plant passionflowers in full sun to partial shade, in soil that is moist but well drained and rich in organic matter. Many tolerate sandy soil, as long as it contains adequate nutrients. Blue passionflower tolerates heavy clay soils and those with an alkaline pH. For blue passion-flower in particular, a sheltered location away from cool winds is helpful, especially in the northern parts of the growing range. Winter mulch is also recom-mended in cooler climates.

Sow seeds or set out nursery plants in spring. Prune in either late fall or early spring to remove dead and damaged wood. To propagate new plants, take cut-tings from established plants in summer.

Uses: Passionflowers are lovely on a trellis, for decoration or as a screen.

Passiflora × *alatocaerulea* is hardy in zone 9 and south. In summer it bears fragrant large flowers of white tinged with pink, with a violet central crown. The lobed leaves are evergreen, and the twining vines can reach 25 feet in length.

Maypop (Passiflora incarnata)

Blue passionflower, *P. caerulea*, climbs by coiling its tendrils around a support, and has deeply lobed leaves. It grows best in zones 8 to 11, although it is often hardy in zone 7 and I have seen it flourishing next to a garage in Pennsylvania, in zone 6. At any rate, this species can tolerate some frost. You can also grow it in a large tub and bring it indoors or into a greenhouse in winter. The large flowers, which can be 4 inches across, are white to pale blue, with a central crown that is purple at the base, white in the middle, and violet at the tip. The flowers appear from early summer to early autumn. The lobed leaves are evergreen in warm climates. Where the warm growing season is long enough the plants produce edible yellow fruit. The cultivar 'Grandi-flora' has larger flowers, to 6 inches across. 'Constance Elliott' has white flowers.

The hardiest of the passionflowers is the maypop, *P. incarnata*. It grows as far north as zone 7 (although a hybrid cultivar, 'Incense', is said to be even hardier, surviving to zone 5). Maypop climbs by tendrils and has deeply lobed, toothed leaves up to 6 inches long. The flowers are white to pale lavender, 2 to 3 inches across, with a pink to purple central crown. In warm climates maypop can bloom for much of the year; farther north it blooms in summer. Edible yellow fruit is produced where the growing season is long enough.

Another warm-climate species, crimson passionflower (*P. vitifolia*), blooms lavishly with flowers of rich crimson. The vines grow to 20 feet, climbing by tendrils, and the green leaves are deeply lobed. Crimson passionflower is suitable only for gardens in zones 10 and 11. It does best in a sunny location.

Pelargonium
IVY GERANIUM

Ivy geranium (*Pelargonium peltatum*) is named for its leaves, which are divided into pointed segments and resemble the foliage of English ivy. Unlike the closely related zonal or bedding geraniums, the ivy geranium has a spreading, trailing habit that is perfectly suited to hanging baskets.

Ivy geraniums produce loose clusters of flowers in white or shades of pink all summer until frost stops them. The trailing stems can grow 3 feet long.

Hardiness: Ivy geranium is a tender perennial that cannot tolerate frost and grows best in warm weather. You can grow it as an annual and discard it at the end of the growing season, or bring it indoors over winter as a houseplant.

Culture: Ivy geraniums grow well in full sun or partial shade, and prefer moist but well-drained soil of average fertility. Water as often as needed to keep the soil evenly moist (but not soggy); the plants will suffer in dry soil.

Deadhead (remove faded flowers) regularly to keep the plants producing more. A biweekly feeding with a liquid all-purpose fertilizer is beneficial during the outdoor growing season.

Move plants outdoors when all danger of frost is past in spring and the weather has warmed. If you want to carry over the plants for a second year, move them indoors before the first fall frost occurs.

Ivy geraniums kept from year to year need pruning to maintain an attractive shape, or you can take cuttings every year or two and start new plants.

Petunia

A true annual, petunias (*Petunia* × *hybrida*) are warm-weather plants with funnel-shaped flowers in many shades of red, rose, pink, purple, lavender-blue, salmon, and white. About the only color not represented (at least not yet) is orange. There are bicolored flowers striped or edges with white, and cultivars with frilled, wavy, ruffled, or doubled flowers. There are different types of hybrid petunias. Grandiflora petunias have the largest, showiest flowers, often ruffled and with doubled petals. Multiflora petunias have smaller, usually single flowers but produce loads of them.

A less common species, *Petunia integrifolia*, has smaller flowers of bright rose-purple, and a vining habit. It will trail or climb if given support. All petunias work fine in hanging baskets, but cascading hybrid varieties and *Petunia integrifolia* are best of all.

Petunias have hairy, sticky stems and leaves. The flowers may be damaged by strong winds and heavy rain, so it's a good idea to move hanging baskets under cover when you expect a summer storm.

The plants bloom happily all summer if you deadhead them frequently. If flowering slows around midsummer, cut back the plants to give them a fresh start.

Hardiness: Petunias are tender annuals that cannot tolerate frost and grow best in warm weather.

Culture: Plant petunias in full sun, in moist but well-drained all-purpose potting mix. They can go outdoors when all danger of frost is past and the weather has warmed in spring. They can tolerate some dryness once established, so water only when the soil becomes dry and the pot feels light when you lift it.

Phaseolus
SCARLET RUNNER BEAN

Scarlet runner bean (*Phaseolus coccineus*) is at home in either the vegetable garden or the flower bed. A twining tender perennial, it is usually grown as an annual, like other garden beans. The vines grow to 10 to 15 feet in the course of a summer, with oval, dark green leaves in groups of three. The brilliant scarlet flowers are showstoppers, and they are a true scarlet (orange-red) color. 'Albus' has white flowers, and those of 'Painted Lady' are salmon and white bicolors. Keep the beans picked to keep the gorgeous flowers coming. The broad, coarse-skinned pods are edible when very young, but the purple-streaked seeds inside are better; let them develop and use them as fresh shell beans.

Hardiness: Scarlet runner bean cannot tolerate any frost, but it grows best where summers are rather cool.

Culture: Give scarlet runner beans full sun and moist but well-drained soil of average fertility. Sow seeds directly in the garden when the danger of frost is past in spring. They need plenty of water in hot, dry weather.

Uses: Plant scarlet runner beans to climb strings or wires, a trellis or latticework, or to cover an arch or arbor.

Polygonum
SILVERLACE VINE

The silverlace or silverfleece vine, *Polygonum aubertii*, is a durable, fast-growing twiner that adapts to a range of conditions. The vines grow quickly to 25 feet or more, with oval to lance-shaped leaves of medium green to 2½ inches long. In late summer to early fall the plants bedeck themselves with lacy sprays of tiny, mildly fragrant white flowers.

Hardiness: Silverlace vine is hardy in zones 5 to 9.

Culture: Silverlace vine needs little in the way of maintenance. It grows well in full sun to partial shade, although it blooms best in sun. The plant tolerates a range of soils, including alkaline ones, and thrives in moist soils of average fertility. It also tolerates dry soil once established, but may not do well in heavy, poorly drained soil. The only pruning needed is to keep the plant in bounds.

Uses: Plant silverlace vine on a trellis, pergola, or an arbor, or use it for screening or quick cover on a chainlink fence. It can also disguise inconveniently placed utility poles and other eyesores.

Rhodochiton
PURPLE BELL VINE

A relatively new addition to mail-order seed catalogs, purple bell vine, *Rhodochiton atrosanguineum* (sometimes listed as *R. volubile*) is a fast-growing tender perennial. The vines grow to 10 feet long, and climb by leaf-stalks. Throughout much of the summer they produce loads of interesting flowers. Tubular flowers of deep blackish purple extend from drooping, bell-shaped calyces of an unusual dusty pinkish maroon color. The green leaves are heart-shaped. The calyces remain for a time after the flowers fall from inside them, and the plant is then covered with bells.

Hardiness: Purple bell vine is perennial only in zones 10 and 11. Gardeners elsewhere can grow it as an annual or bring it indoors in winter to a cool, bright room.

Culture: Plant purple bell vine in full sun to partial shade, in any average well-drained soil. You can start seeds indoors in early spring, six to eight weeks before you expect to plant them out. Do not move plants outdoors until all danger of frost is past and the soil has warmed.

If you plan to move a potted plant indoors for winter, get it inside before the first fall frost.

Uses: Grow purple bell vine in a hanging basket, or train it on a trellis or a topiary ring form. It is also attractive against a fence, or when allowed to sprawl as a groundcover.

Rosa
CLIMBING ROSES
RAMBLER ROSES

Climbing roses (*Rosa* hybrids) are not true vines; they are rambling shrubs with long stems that are unable to climb without help from the gardener. Basically, the plants just send their stems upward. The stems either come to rest on a convenient support or arc over and hit the ground. Attaching the long canes to a trellis, arbor, or other support allows them to grow vertically and show off their beautiful blossoms. But for the best bloom, fan out the stems and fasten them in a more horizontal position on a fence or other support. Climbing roses have somewhat stiff canes and produce their flowers singly or in clusters. Most bloom in early summer and often again in fall. Some of the best climbing roses are 'New Dawn', 'Dorothy Perkins', 'Blaze', 'Dortmund', 'Gloire de Dijon', and 'Climbing Peace'.

Purple bell vine (Rhodochiton atrosanguineum)

Rambler roses are quite like climbing roses. Their canes are more flexible and they bear their small flowers in clusters and a bit later than climbers, in midsummer. They do not rebloom in autumn. Rambler roses are lovely trained on a rail fence or woven through a trellis or lattice screen. 'American Pillar' is one good variety.

Hardiness: Hardiness varies, but many climbing and rambler roses are hardy in zones 5 to 9.

Culture: Like other roses, climbers and ramblers need full sun—at least six hours of un-obstructed sun a day—and soil that is moist but well drained and rich in organic matter, with a slightly acid to neutral pH. Roses suffer in soil that is too light and porous; add lots of organic matter to sandy soils to improve the texture and water-holding capacity.

Rosa 'American Pillar'

Plant bare-root plants in spring or fall, and container-grown plants anytime during the growing season when weather conditions are mild and not too stressful.

Train climbing and rambler roses by tying strong, flexible canes loosely to the support with soft twine, long twist ties, or other material. Right after plants bloom is a good time to begin training new canes. When plants are several years old, prune them to remove any dead or damaged wood, and cut one-third of the oldest canes back to the ground to make room for vigorous new growth.

Feed roses monthly during the growing season with a balanced all-purpose fertilizer. Top-dress with compost once a year to maintain a high level of organic matter in the soil. Mulching will help to conserve soil moisture.

Hybrid roses are notoriously susceptible to attack from pests and diseases. Good air circulation is an important aid in minimizing mildew problems. Consult your County Cooperative Extension office or a good book on roses for advice on combating pests and diseases.

In the northernmost parts of the growing range, protect the vines from cold winter weather. In late autumn, carefully detach the canes from their supports, and lay them on the ground. Cover with a mound of soil or a layer of shredded leaves or hay 1 foot deep.

Uses: The best means of support for climbing and rambler roses are arbors and arches, pergolas, trellises, pillars, and wooden fences. They are lovely as a backdrop in a sunny flower garden, or trained over the roof of a shed or outbuilding. Climbing roses will also drape their long stems over a retaining wall or terrace to beautiful effect.

Sanvitalia
CREEPING ZINNIA

This diminutive annual is a charming addition to hanging baskets and small gardens. Creeping zinnia (*Sanvitalia procumbens*) has small yellow daisy flowers with large, purple-brown centers— they actually look like miniature sunflowers rather than zinnias.

The thin, trailing stems with their small, oval leaves stay close to the ground—plants rarely grow more than 6 inches high.

Hardiness: Creeping zinnia is a tender perennial that cannot tolerate frost and grows best in warm weather.

Culture: Do not plant out creeping zinnia until all danger of frost is past in spring. Direct-sow or, in cool climates, sow indoors in peat pots about six weeks before the last frost date. Press seeds lightly into the soil but do not cover them; they germinate better when exposed to light.

Give creeping zinnia a location in full sun, in soil that is light and well drained, and of average fertility. The plants generally endure hot, humid weather with no problem.

Uses: Plant creeping zinnia in the front of a small flower bed or border, or let its stems dangle over the sides of a hanging basket or windowbox.

Schizophragma
JAPANESE HYDRANGEA VINE

As its common name implies, Japanese hydrangea vine (*Schizophragma hydrageoides*) is an oriental plant that is similar in appearance to climbing hydrangea. Japanese hydrangea vine clings by sticky rootlike structures on its stems to reach a height of 18 feet or more. It has broad, oval leaves

of deep green, growing to 4 inches long, with toothed edges; they are smaller than the leaves of climbing hydrangea.
In midsummer there are flat-topped clusters of white flowers that somewhat resemble the blossoms of lacecap hydrangeas. The cultivar 'Moonlight' has especially lovely foliage in addition to its flowers; the bluish green leaves have dark green tracery around the veins.

Hardiness: Japanese hydrangea vine is hardy in zones 5 to 7.

Culture: This vine grows well in partial to light shade, but also tolerates full sun. The plant prefers soil that is fertile and evenly moist.

Set out young plants in spring, and cut back the stems after planting to 6 to 8 inches, to encourage bushier growth. To propagate new plants, take softwood cuttings or layer a low stem.

Uses: Japanese hydrangea vine is a good choice to climb a tree trunk or masonry wall, or to camouflage boulders and other undesirable landscape features that would be difficult to remove.

Stephanotis
MADAGASCAR JASMINE

The intensely fragrant flowers of stephanotis, sometimes called Madagascar jasmine (*Stephanotis floribunda*), are a popular part of many bridal bouquets and Hawaiian leis. The twining vine grows to 15 feet or more, with glossy, dark green, evegreen, elliptical leaves to 4 inches long. In summer the plant bears clusters of tubular, sweet-scented waxy white flowers. The heavy perfume of the blossoms is over-powering to some noses and exquisite to others.

Hardiness: Stephanotis is hardy only in the frost-free climates or zones 10 and 11, although garden-ers farther north can grow it in a pot moved indoors in winter.

Culture: Give Madagascar jasmine a location where the vine receives sun for half the day but the roots are shaded. Good air circulation is important, especially in summer, and the plant can take a bit more shade at that time of year, too. Plant in fertile, humusy, well-drained soil or rich potting mix that is kept evenly moist during the spring and summer. Cut back on watering and do not fertilize during fall and winter to allow the plant to rest.

Prune in spring to thin out crowded stems or shorten stems that are too long. Start new plants from seed in spring or semihardwood cuttings taken in summer.

Uses: Grow Madagascar jasmine on a trellis near a window or patio, where you can drink in the luxurious fragrance.

Tecomaria
CAPE HONEYSUCKLE

A very vigorous climbing or rambling shrub for warm climates, Cape honeysuckle (*Tecomaria capensis*) grows to 20 feet or more. Plants have compound, light green, evergreen leaves to 6 inches long; the rounded, glossy green leaflets have toothed edges. From late summer into winter there are clusters of brilliant red-orange funnel-shaped flowers about 2 inches long. There are yellow-flowered culti-vars as well, 'Aurea' and 'Lutea', which may actually be two differ-ent names for the same variety. Hardiness: Cape honeysuckle is hardy in zones 8 to 11.

Culture: Tecomaria grows well in light, sandy soils, with plenty of sun. You can also grow Cape honeysuckle in a tub and bring it indoors to spend the winter in a cool, bright place with tem-peratures of 40° to 50° F. In a container give the plant a rich, fertile, well-drained potting mix. Water deeply during dry weather. The topgrowth may die back in cold winter weather where the plant is hardy, but it will regrow in spring.

Prune plants in spring only to remove dead wood and keep the growth under control. Propagate new plants from seed, cuttings, root cuttings, or layering.

Uses: Grow Cape honeysuckle as a vine, or prune it and use it as a shrub or a hedge. Another option is to let the shrubs ramble over a slope.

Thunbergia
BLACK-EYED SUSAN VINE

A twining tender perennial, black-eyed Susan vine or clock vine (*Thunbergia alata*), is grown as an annual north of zone 10. The trailing vines grow to 6 feet, and can be trained to climb by attaching them to a trellis. Plants have oval to triangular leaves with toothed edges. In mid- to late summer black-eyed Susan vine produces gold, orange, or ivory flowers with wide, flat petals and a dark center. In warm climates the plants often bloom for much of the year. Several cultivars are available: 'Alba' has all creamy white flowers, 'Aurantiaca' has yellow-orange flowers, and 'Susy Mixed' has flowers in yellow, orange, and white.

A seldom seen close relative of black-eyed Susan vine is the Bengal clock vine or sky flower, *Thunbergia grandiflora*. Also a tender perennial twiner, Bengal clock vine is hardy in mild climates and treated as an annual farther north. This vine has larger leaves than its relative; they are oval, and as much as 8 inches long. The flowers, too, are different. Sky blue flowers about 3 inches across with pale yellow tubular throats are produced in drooping clusters in mid- to late summer in northern gardens, in mid-spring and sporadically throughout much of the year where the plant is perennial.

Hardiness: Black-eyed Susan vine is tender; it cannot tolerate frost and grows best in warm weather. Grow it as an annual in all but frost-free climates. Bengal clock vine is hardy in zones 9 to 11, and in sheltered locations in zone 8.

*Bengal clock vine (*Thunbergia grandiflora*)*

Culture: Black-eyed Susan vine grows best in warm weather, in fertile, moist but well-drained soil. It will tolerate sandy soil. Give it a location in full sun to light shade. In zones 10 and 11, sow seeds outdoors when the weather warms in early spring. Elsewhere, start seeds indoors and transplant outside when the danger of frost is past.

Plant Bengal clock vine in partial to light shade, in fertile, moist but well-drained soil rich in organic matter, or an all-purpose potting mix. Planting directions are the same as those given above for black-eyed Susan vine.

Uses: Grow black-eyed Susan vine to climb a trellis or strings, or let it dangle from hanging baskets. Bengal clock vine is also delightful in a hanging basket, or in warmer climes trained up a trellis or an arbor, or around a porch.

Nasturtium (Tropaeolum majus)

Trachelospermum
CONFEDERATE JASMINE

An evergreen vine from China, Confederate jasmine (*Trachelospermum jasminoides*) got its common name from its long history in southeastern gardens. The plant is also known as star jasmine. Confederate jasmine is a vigorous twiner that grows quickly to 15 feet or more. It has small, oblong to elliptical, evergreen leaves that are dark green in color. In spring and early summer the plant bears clusters of intensely fragrant, star-shaped tubular-throated flowers of creamy white. There is one cultivar, 'Variegatum', with green and white variegated leaves, and another, 'Japonicum', whose leaves are veined in white and turn bronze in autumn.

Hardiness: Confederate jasmine is hardy in zones 8 to 11.

Culture: Give the plant a cool, sunny or lightly shady location with evenly moist soil. It usually takes two or three years to become established, so give it time. Prune the plant to keep it under control.

Uses: Confederate jasmine is excellent for screening or covering a trellis. Locate it where you can enjoy the scent when the plants are blooming. You can also plant trachelospermum as a groundcover, and let it sprawl over a slope.

Tropaeolum
NASTURTIUM

If you are used to seeing nasturtiums (*Tropaeolum majus*) tumbling about along the edges of flower gardens, or scattered on top of your salad, you probably don't think of them as vines. But their long stems will trail from a hanging basket or, with a little help, climb strings, wires, or a trellis. The stems of nasturtiums (the traditional kind, not dwarf cultivars) grow as long as 8 feet. The unusual leaves are disk-shaped and dark green, with lighter veins. The lightly fragrant flowers are funnel-shaped, with five wide petals and a curved spur. They come in warm tones of red, mahogany, orange, gold, yellow, and white, and bloom all summer. Both the leaves and flowers are edible, with a peppery flavor similar to watercress (to which nasturtiums are closely related). The buds are sometimes pickled in sour brine and used as substitutes for capers.

Hardiness: Nasturtiums are tender annuals that cannot tolerate frost, but they grow best where summers are not extremely hot and humid.

Culture: Give nasturtiums full sun to partial shade, and well-drained sandy or gritty soil of average or even poor fertility. In rich soil, especially soil with a high nitrogen content, plants tend to produce luxuriant foliage but not many flowers. Nasturtiums do not transplant well, and are best sown directly where you want them to grow. Sow when all danger of frost is past and the soil warms in spring.

Aphids are attracted to nasturtiums, so check for them often, especially around young shoot tips and in leaf axils. Spray with insecticidal soap if you discover an infestation.

Before the first fall frost, you can take cuttings of young shoots and root them in pots for winter houseplants. Give indoor plants as much sun as possible.

Uses: Nasturtiums trained to climb strings make a colorful screen at the back of the garden. You can also grow them on a trellis or let them ramble about among rocks or over a gentle slope. Or grow them in hanging baskets.

Tropaeolum
CANARY CREEPER

This nasturtium relative, known to botanists as *Tropaeolum peregrinum*, is a twining annual vine growing to 10 feet. The attractive, light green leaves have several rounded lobes like fingers on a hand. Throughout much of the summer, the small, bright yellow fringed flowers look like tiny birds perched among the leaves. Like nasturtiums, they are edible and taste peppery.

Hardiness: Canary creeper is a tender annual that cannot tolerate frost.

Culture: Give this vine a location in full sun to partial shade, with average soil. It grows best where summers are not intensely hot. Sow seeds directly in the garden when all danger of frost is past in spring and the soil is warm.

Uses: Canary creeper is an excellent plant to cover a chain link fence, or to grow on a trellis, post, or vertical strings or wires. For an unusual effect, plant the vine near an evergreen shrub or hedge where it can weave its flowering stems through the larger plant. You can also use it as a groundcover.

Verbena

Garden verbena (*Verbena × hybrida*) is a popular annual for gardens and containers. It offers round clusters of dainty little flowers of red, pink, rose, purple, and white that bloom for most of the summer, and sometimes into fall. The dark green, oval to lance-shaped leaves have notched or toothed edges. Many garden verbenas are small, upright plants about a foot high, but there are also trailing varieties that make terrific hanging basket plants.

Another species, *Verbena peruviana*, creeps across the ground, its stems rooting where the nodes touch the ground. It also has upright stems up to 2 feet tall. This species also has clusters of flowers, bright red in this case, and toothed dark green leaves.

Hardiness: Both species described here are tender annuals that cannot tolerate frost.

Culture: Verbenas grow best in warm weather and should not go into the garden until all danger of frost is past in spring. Seeds can be difficult to germinate, so start with nursery plants if you can find them locally. If you do wish to start from seed, sow early indoors or in a coldframe, in light, porous, well-drained soil.

In southern locations where the summer sun is intense, give verbena a spot where it will receive some light shade in the afternoon. Elsewhere plant in full sun, in average, well-drained soil.

Don't let the soil become extremely dry between waterings; verbena suffers if it gets too dry.

Verbena is prone to mildew and leaf miners. Allow good air circulation between and around plants to help reduce mildew problems, and remove immediately any leaves that show the pale tracery of leafminer tunnels.

Uses: Both species of verbena are excellent hanging basket plants. *V. peruviana* is also charming when allowed to trail along the front of a garden bed or border.

Vinca

PERIWINKLE

There are two species of vinca, both of which are popular—and deservedly so—among American gardeners. Periwinkle or myrtle, *Vinca minor*, is an attractive, versatile groundcover that grows well in sun or shade. The vines creep across the ground and form roots at various points along the stem. The plants spread fairly quickly to carpet an area. They have glossy, evergreen, oval leaves about 2 inches long. In early spring blue-violet flowers quite similar in color to the periwinkle crayon in a box of crayons appear. Vinca has been grown in American gardens since Colonial days, and in some areas it has escaped from cultivation to live in the wild.

In addition to the species form, several cultivars are available. 'Alba' has white flowers, those of 'Atropurpurea' are purple, and 'Bowles Variety' has light blue flowers and a less spreading habit of growth.

An upright-growing species with similar-looking flowers of pink or white is Madagascar periwinkle, *Catharanthus roseus*. Although in some places this plant is also called vinca, it is not a true vinca.

Greater periwinkle, *Vinca major*, is less hardy than *Vinca minor*, with larger, wider leaves of a lighter shade of green. It's a popular groundcover in some areas along the West Coast, and indispensable in windowboxes, hanging baskets, and planters all over the country. The triangular leaves are about 2 inches long. The bluish purple flowers are very similar to those of periwinkle, but a bit larger, and they bloom in mid-spring. The most often grown form is a variegated cultivar, 'Variegata' (sometimes called 'Elegantissima'), which has leaves irregularly edged in creamy pale yellow.

Hardiness: Periwinkle is hardy in zones 4 or 5 to 9, greater periwinkle in zones 7 to 9.

Culture: Vinca thrives in full sun to moderate shade. It is not fussy about soil, although it grows and spreads more rapidly in soils of good fertility. Periwinkle does not take well to dry conditions, and needs soil that can retain moisture but is not soggy. Soil rich in organic matter is ideal. Water during spells of dry weather.

Canary Creeper (Tropaeolum peregrinum)

Periwinkle is easily propagated by division, since its creeping stems root at numerous places along their length. Cut apart rooted sections and transplant them to get vinca started in a new location.

The plants are not harmed by shearing, and you can clip them back when they get out of hand to keep them in place and looking neat.

Uses: Plant vinca as a ground-cover under trees and shrubs, or on a bank. Set plant 12 to 18 inches apart. Greater periwinkle also makes a good groundcover where it is hardy, and is an excellent trailer for hanging baskets and other containers.

Periwinkle (Vinca minor)

Vitis
GRAPES

If you need shade fast in a sunny yard that was cleared of trees when your house was built, one good way to get it is to put up an arbor and plant grapevines to cover it. Grapes grow quickly, and their large, lobed leaves are good at casting shade.

One of the best kinds of grapes to plant on an arbor is a species with decorative fall foliage, aptly named crimson glory vine, *Vitis coignetiae.*

Grapevines are deciduous vines that climb by wrapping their tendrils around a support. Horizontal supports are easiest for the tendrils to grasp. In vineyards, grapes are trained on trellises made of three or more horizontal strands of heavy wire. The long vines need to be fastened to vertical supports in order to climb them.

Grapes produce inconspicuous flowers that are not ornamental, but which are fragrant in some species.

Crimson glory vine is native to Japan and grows quickly, sometimes as much as 50 feet in a single growing season. The more-or-less heart-shaped leaves have irregularly toothed edges and may grow up to 10 inches across. In fall they turn brilliant red. The vines produce clusters of blue-black fruit.

There are also grapes native to different parts of North America that are easy to grow in appropriate locations. Along the West Coast there is the California grape, *V. californica.* The fox grape, *V. labrusca,* grows wild in the eastern U.S., from Georgia up to New England. Two other eastern species are the river-bank grape, *V. riparia,* and frost grape, *V. vulpina.* Muscadines (*V. rotundifolia*) are native to the Southeast and lower Midwest.

Hardiness: Crimson glory vine is hardy in zones 5 to 11.

Culture: For ornamental purposes you can plant grapes in full sun to partial or even light shade. They grow best in porous, well-drained soil but some, particularly crimson glory vine, tolerate heavier clay soils as well.

Water grapes during periods of dry weather.

Most grapevines are easy to propagate from cuttings or layering. Take cuttings in spring. Each cutting should include a bud and an inch or two of healthy stem from last year's growth both above and below the bud. Plant the cutting in a pot of moist, sandy soil with the bud sitting right on top of the soil.

Cuttings of crimson glory vine will not root well so this species is best started from nursery plants, or seeds that have been stratified (given cold temperatures of 40° F) for three months.

Uses: In addition to providing shade, grapes are useful for screening, or to cover a ram-shackle shed or other eyesore. You can also let them ramble across a steep slope or other area that is difficult to maintain.

Wisteria

The fragrant flowers of wisteria are pure delight in mid- to late spring. It's too bad the vines that produce them can get so out of hand. If you intend to grow wisteria, plan on pruning every year to keep it under control. For those of us who love the sweet-scented flowers, the extra work is well worthwhile.

Growing wisteria is not a short-term process. Wisteria takes a long time to begin blooming; plants sometimes wait ten years or more to produce their first flowers.

There are numerous native wisteria species, but the two grown for ornamental purposes are both from the Orient. Both are woody twining vines whose deciduous compound leaves consist of opposite pairs of oval leaflets. The leaves turn an attractive yellow in autumn before they fall. The vines bear long, drooping flower clusters in spring. Japanese wisteria (*Wisteria floribunda*) grows to 25 feet, twining its stems in a clockwise direction, and is the hardier of the two. The leaves contain more leaflets (thirteen to nineteen) than those of Chinese wisteria. Japanese wisteria also has the longer and more fragrant flower clusters—they are often 18 inches long. The variety *macro-botrys* has even longer clusters of flowers, to 3 or sometimes even 4 feet. The species has pealike flowers of a light violet color, but cultivars are available with white, pink, red, or deeper violet blossoms. The flowers of both wisteria species are followed in summer by long, flat, velvety green seedpods that dangle from the stems.

Chinese wisteria (*W. sinensis*) grows to 30 feet in length, twines in a counterclockwise direction, and blooms a week or two ahead of the Japanese species. Its lightly fragrant blue-violet flowers come in clusters 8 to 12 inches long. The cultivar 'Alba' has more fragrant, white flowers; those of 'Purpurea' are violet-purple.

Hardiness: Japanese wisteria is hardy in zones 4 to 9. Chinese wisteria grows in zones 5 to 10.

Culture: Wisteria flowers best in full sun but will also grow in partial shade. It needs fertile soil that is rich in organic matter and moist but well drained. It will also tolerate heavier clay soils, and soil with an alkaline pH. Abundant moisture is especially important during wisteria's first year in the garden.

Transplant wisteria with care; like all legumes, its roots resent being disturbed. Fasten the young stems to their support until the vines are able to twine around on their own.

To keep the soil humusy, mulch plants with compost or composted manure in fall. Work the organic material into the soil in spring, being careful to not damage the roots.

Pruning: Wisteria needs regular pruning to look its best, and to remain within bounds. In summer, prune all the long, straggly stems that develop, except for the ones the vine needs to climb. Also shorten the lateral stems. Cut back stems being pruned by one-third to one-half their length, to produce the best flowers. In late winter, before new growth begins, prune again, cutting back the previously pruned shoots to two or three buds. Cut back to 6 inches any long shoots that developed after last summer's pruning.

Uses: Wisteria is lovely trained on an arbor or pergola, on a fence, or on a sturdy trellis. It is dense enough to use for screening. It will also climb a tree trunk or even the wall of a building. For a formal treatment, you can, over a period of years, train wisteria to take the form of a tree. A lot of pruning is required to achieve the form. Allow one main stem to develop and support it with stakes until it is sturdy

enough to stand by itself. Careful pruning and training of lateral stems will allow you to develop a canopy of foliage and flowers atop the main stem. Over time, the stems of wisteria become thick, woody, and interestingly gnarled and twisted.

When Wisteria Won't Bloom: If your wisteria doesn't flower, ask yourself the following questions.

Is the plant old enough? Wisteria often takes six or seven years to produce its first flowers, and may take even longer.

Is the soil too rich? Very fertile soil, especially soil rich in nitrogen, causes lavish foliage growth but no flowers. as a remedy, try digging a trench around the base of the plant and working in superphosphate or other phosphorus fertilizer to balance the excess of nitrogen.

An older, more labor-intensive way to stimulate bloom is to prune the roots. Push the sharp blade of a spade into the soil in a circle around the base of the plant to cut the roots. Work about 1½ feet out from the trunk. Severely pruning long stems (back to two or three buds) may also help.

Is there enough light? Wisteria needs a sunny location.

Was last winter too cold? Low temperatures may kill flower buds. If you are in an exposed location or live near the northern boundary of zone 4 or 5, you can try removing the vines from their support and laying them out on the ground in fall. Cover with a foot-deep layer of hay, leaves, or evergreen boughs, or a mound of soil.

*Japanese wisteria (*Wisteria floribunda*)*

Index

96